TIED T
APRO

By

STEWART M. L. POLLARD

Edited by

Lewis C. Wes Cook

MACOY PUBLISHING & MASONIC SUPPLY CO., INC.

Richmond, Virginia

Macoy Publishing & Masonic Supply Co., Inc.
Richmond, Virginia

ISBN-0-88053-059-6

Foreword

Masonic research far too often leaves the impression that the curious student who enters the quarries will find only questions and answers of a serious nature. Far from the truth!

There are tears of joy as well as sadness. There are embarrassed, reluctant smiles; smiles that warm the heart as we share in the good fortune of others or the stimulating remarks they have brought to our lodge rooms; quiet chuckles when a Brother in his concern and nervousness accidentally gets his ritual work upside down or backwards, or gets his feet all tangled while trying to remember just exactly where the lecturer told him to place them.

Tied to Masonic Apron Strings shows another side of Freemasonry. It brings us together with some old friends and some new and gives us an opportunity to laugh at ourselves and with our Brethren. There are moments, too, when the poet paints the canvas with words that reflect all of the beauty of our Fraternity from its rich, fertile valleys to its snow-capped peaks that reach out to touch the clouds and share in a unique communion with the Master Architect.

The Missouri Lodge of Research feels that sometimes we take ourselves too seriously as Masons. Thanks to Stewart M. L. Pollard, with an assist from cartoons made available through the generous cooperation of William R. Denslow, editor of *The Royal Arch Mason* Magazine, we hope to produce an endless string of quiet chuckles and warm smiles, and occasionally a tug at your heart strings, as you read *Tied to Masonic Apron Strings*.

HAROLD N. PAINTER
Master
Missouri Lodge of Research, 1968-69

Preface

Hillside, Maryland
September 1969 AD
AL5969

Probably the biggest joke in this collection is that it *started out* to be a booklet of Masonic *humor*.

It was my pleasure in February 1967 to attend sessions of the Grand Masters Conference in Washington, D.C. It was there, listening to these grand old Masons spin yarns about Masonry that I realized what a wealth of humorous material there was on the subject.

Procrastination, lodge meetings, and military duties seemed to keep me from doing anything about it for several months. By then I had forgotten the stories I had heard—but remembered they'd been funny. Dashing off letters to some of the Grand Masters who had been at the conference didn't bring in much material. Encouragement—Yes! But, jokes, stories and humorous incidents—No! These appear to be included in their vows of secrecy! To those who did contribute, I offer my sincere thanks!

Thanks to the encouragement of M.W. Bro. William R. Denslow, of *The Royal Arch Mason,* I was put in touch with Bro. Wes Cook, Editor for The Missouri Lodge of Research, who added the right spark of inspiration for me to dig further into the quarries where humor abounds. But, there was so much seriousness in even the "lighter side" of Masonry that instead of items for a book of humor, I was gathering material of inspirational character, too. There was so much similarity in the Masonic "jokes"—or because of their lack of taste they were not usable—it soon became evident that I was not going to have enough material for a book of humor that anyone would read.

Well, then Uncle Sam came along with the idea that my military talents were needed in the Republic of China. So off I went to beautiful Taiwan, expecting to have plenty of time to pursue my humorous quarrying, but instead finding myself totally engrossed in one of the outstanding Masonic adventures of my life. (If you want to see Masonry-in-action, I highly recommend a trip to Taipei.)

Returning to the States, I regrouped my conglomeration of "humor," weeded out the sick jokes (most of them); purged many of the stories involving race, creed, religion, and sex; added some educational material, together with inspirational items and came up with what you'll find on the following pages.

In most instances, I have indicated *my* source—although many items have origins unknown—having been published elsewhere. While there are a few "rib ticklers" in this collection, I hope you'll find many that will "tickle your fancy" as they did mine.

DEDICATION

I have three great loves! My family! The U.S. Army! And Masonry!

Already dedicated to my family—the dedication of a book to them would be superfluous. Therefore, I should like to dedicate this volume to my brethren of

NATIONAL SOJOURNERS, INC.,

an organization composed of my comrades-at-arms who are Master Masons.

Fraternally and Zealously,
STEWART M. L. POLLARD

TIED TO MASONIC APRON STRINGS

I

"Wrinkles should merely indicate where smiles have been."

(MARK TWAIN)

BLOOPER

A well-known radio-announcer, who must remain unidentified (until he is fired), was reading his *Trestleboard* just prior to a station break. Subconsciously, and apparently unnoticed, he announced, "This is radio-station KVZ, AF and AM." (The station letters are fictitious to protect the guilty.)

NEITHER SHOULD GRAVES

A brother died July 18, 1931. His lodge was opened in due form, but when the funeral was over the lodge was not closed. Only three brethren had returned to the hall—not enough to close the lodge, and according to the complaint "the lodge is still open; over a month has transpired."

The grand master, somewhat of a humorist, replied:

"Care should be taken with lodges; they should not be allowed to lay around *open,* indiscriminately."

HIGH FINANCE

Missouri's Ryland Lodge, in 1904, was reported to have raised their dues to pay for their hall, but later declared dividends out of the funds on hand. Another lodge, before surrendering its charter had paid each brother a "dividend." Masonic corporations? Stock dividend?

UNDERSTANDING

In 1913, a grand master was asked to decide upon the validity of a petition signed by one "who had feet of unequal size." (We wonder if the *Army* rejected him in 1918.)

KNOCK-KNOCK

And a former grand lecturer was once asked "which of several knocks should be given first?"

"Do you like it? Cost me a squaw and two of my best horses."

THE GREAT LIGHTS

In answer to the question of what the DeMolay expects from Masons, DeMolay leaders at the 46th Annual Session of the International Supreme Council of the Order of DeMolay answered: "We would rather see your shiny bald heads than your shiny silver dollars." They had other sage comments, too, but this seems to be the best starting point.

POLITICAL GALLOWS

In the heat of a political campaign two Masonic brothers found themselves on opposite sides of the political fence. One caused the other to be hanged in effigy from the limb of a tree in front of a railroad station. The offended brother brought Masonic charges and the offender was brought to trial, but acquitted. Such political differences, it was held, will not support Masonic charges.

(Wor. Everett Howser)

KEEPING UP WITH THE JONES

Green City Lodge No. 159 once reported that a defendant had been acquitted of charges because:

(a) Since his expulsion by grand lodge, he has been acquitted by the Odd Fellows.

(b) He has since been acquitted by the Baptist Church.

TRIPPING THROUGH THE GRAVEYARD

Marcus Lodge No. 110 reported the loss of its charter which had been kept in a sacred—if not secure—place—"between the leaves of the Bible."

On the way to the cemetery for the burial of a brother, the old Bible-bearer tripped, spilling the Three Great Lights, and spreading the Gospel and Charter to the four quarters of the earth.

For the information of the committee and the grand master, it was explained:

The Bible-bearer was not intoxicated as he was a minister of the Gospel.

Just *what* Gospel deponent saith not.

BROTHER

B e ready with a friendly greeting,
R eserve night when we hold meetings,
O bey the Master's pleas and wishes,
T ake time to help out with the dishes,
H elp widows, orphans, with quickness,
E ase, too, the lot of those with sickness
R emember to love one another—
—and you'll deserve the name of
BROTHER

(Walter K. Belt, P.M.)

BEST WISHES

May the cause of Brotherhood
'Round the World be understood;
And peace espoused in every land,
By one and all on every hand.
May the joys of friendships be renewed,
Greed, and lust, and avarice subdued.
May the good which can be done,
Touch the lives of everyone.
May the gifts which we possess,
Be deployed for happiness.

(R.W. Cyril E. Brubaker)

OBEY THAT IMPULSE!

The secret of expressing appreciation *effectively* is to do something about it as soon as the impulse hits you. Don't wait, don't put it off! If you feel that somebody has done a good job, if you feel grateful to somebody for something—tell him so—immediately. Don't let the warm spot in your heart cool. Praise is like whipped cream; it should be served freshly whipped.

What that much TV-ed tonic is supposed to do for tired blood, praise will do for a tired spirit. People hunger for appreciation—your family, your friends, your business associates. Praise may embarrass them a bit—coming from you!—but they will love it. Under the sunshine of your *expressed* appreciation their personalities will blossom in a way that will amaze you. And *you* will do a little blossoming yourself!

(*The Little Gazette*)

THE ENTERED APPRENTICE

By Bro. Wilbur D. Nesbit

They made me an Entered Apprentice; they gave me my first degree;
They gave me the base for an honest pride, and took some conceit from me.
I thought I should have attendants whose station and rank were high,
That they who should give me instructions would cater to such as I—
So they made me an Entered Apprentice; and good were the words they said;
Their speech was the speech of wisdom, the lore of the heart and head.

And one was an humble person, a man of the everyday,
Whom oft I had passed by proudly on meeting him in my way.
He spoke, and my bigness dwindled, and out of the circling sky
There seemed to come down a message for me to be measured by.
I got me a newer learning, an inkling of some great plan—
They made me an Entered Apprentice in the building of a man.

And one was a kindly scholar whom many a day I'd seen,
With speech that was firm, yet gentle, and countenance all serene;
He taught me a wealth of learning that never was yet in schools
And showed me the grief they garner that walk in the way of fools.

The simple, eternal precepts they put in my mind and heart—
They made me an Entered Apprentice and bade me to do my part.

They made me an Entered Apprentice—I was not so proud a man,
A pride that was deeper, newer, that all meaner things must ban
Took place of the old vainglory, and all for my soul's own good,
As dimly the patient teachings began to be understood.
They made me an Entered Apprentice; they gave me my first degree;
They gave me the base for a decent pride, and took some conceit from me.

NO STRANGERS HERE

Over the Tyler's station in Howard Lodge No. 101, Maryland, of which Bro. W. Norman Penn, Most Worshipful Grand Master of Maryland, is a member, is a sign which reads:

"THERE ARE NO STRANGERS HERE; YOU ARE AMONG FRIENDS YOU HAVE NOT AS YET MET."

Can you think of any more wonderful way to express the Philosophy, the Spirit, and the Fellowship which we all find in the Fraternity?

"My husband's an active Mason who loves golf. . . . So I'll let you decide when's the best time to catch him in!"

WORRYWARTS

Living is so complicated these days, folks don't even worry right. For instance:

WE WORRY about the Russians, then get run over by a neighbor's car.

WE WORRY about radio-active fallout, then get poisoned by nicotine or by spraying the flowers.

WE WORRY about the youngsters running in front of cars, then drag them across the street against the warning of the red light.

WE WORRY about dwindling lodge attendance and then miss six meetings in a row.

WE WORRY about crashing in an airplane, then fall off a ladder painting the house.

WE WORRY about getting enough exercise, then drive two blocks for a cup of coffee.

WE WORRY about getting the car greased every thousand miles, then never get a medical check-up.

WE WORRY about retirement, then go about carelessly to keep from lasting that long.

WE WORRY about H-bombs, then blow our heads off by smoking around gasoline.

WE WORRY about polio, then get crippled by running into a power lawn mower.

WE WORRY about tornadoes, then get liquidated in a traffic accident.

(Borrowed)

GEORGIA PEACHES

The *Proceedings of the Grand Lodge of Georgia* for 1961 reported some troublesome disciplinary cases. The Grand Master caused charges to be brought against dimitted brethren who had engaged in the liquor business. The Grotto again got into trouble over gambling, was taken to task by the Grand Master, and promised to behave itself in the future. A more serious case involved one of the largest lodges in Georgia, which, as a joke, introduced a live pig escorted by two clowns into the lodge-room, for initiation in the E.A. Degree. This, with the lodge opened and the Great Lights displayed! The Grand Master was outspoken in his condemnation. He summoned the entire membership to a special meeting, at which the lodge was officially reprimanded.

"*When Harry makes a contribution, he doesn't fool around!*"

BEAUTY AID

The Unity of Masons does not come from dull conformity, but rather from the creative talents of each Mason, expressed in various ways, and applied to the task of adding beauty to the Temple of Masonry.

(*Masonic Messenger*)

RUSTOLEUM

Masonry, whether it be structural or speculative, needs most to have action. Machines—human, mechanical or fraternal—will rust out in far less time than they will wear out.

(Alberta, *G. L. Bulletin*)

BANG AWAY

Back in 1879, a dispute arose in a California lodge when a brother refused to obey the Master's gavel and in effect told him, "Bang away all you please! I'm going to have my say!"

He also suggested if the Master didn't want to listen to him, he could turn his chair over to the Senior Warden and leave.

The disputing brother was tried and expelled.

(Southern Calif. Research Lodge)

CHIEF GAWHEGA

Wor. Bro. Stacy Howell (GAWHEGA), a full-blooded Pawnee Indian was installed as Worshipful Master of Bent Lodge No. 42 in Taos, New Mexico, in December 1968.

Howell is the oldest son descendant of Chief GAWHEGA of the Pumpkin-Vine Clan of the Skeedee Pawnee of Oklahoma.

(*The New Mexico Freemason*)

FROM REFRESHMENT TO LABOR AGAIN

Vacation time is over,
Summer has come and gone;
We return to our labors refreshed,
To the work that needs to be done.
We take up the Chisel and Mallet,
The Square, the Level, and Plumb;
Working our trade as Masons,
Doing all tasks as they come.
No shirkers or drones among us,
No duties or chores do we shun;
There is much that needs our attention,
For a Mason's work is never done.

(R.W. CYRIL E. BRUBAKER)

HE REVEALS FREEMASONRY

The brother I write about does not go about shouting his Masonry, yet he reveals the teachings and principles of the Institution.

In his business dealings he always acts on the square.

He walks in quiet dignity. What he has, he willingly shares with others less fortunate, not because he seeks praise, or fears criticism, but just because he knows the joy of sharing.

He is never too busy to say a kind word. He is always too busy to indulge in idle gossip.

He believes in the glorious destiny of America. He is willing to speak out boldly and is not ashamed of being a patriotic citizen.

He is forever conscious of his Divine Heritage and strives to make religion and life one.

What is Masonry? It is what this brother lives.

(DEWEY H. WOLLSTEIN, PGM, in the *Masonic Messenger*)

HOME SWEET HOME

A London magazine sent out 1,000 inquiries on the question, "What is Home?" In selecting the classes to respond to the question it was particular to see that every one was represented. The poorest and the richest were given an equal opportunity to express their sentiments. Out of 800 replies received, seven gems were selected as follows:

Home—A world of strife shut out, a world of love shut in.

Home—The place where the small are great and the great are small.

Home—The father's kingdom, the mother's world, and the child's paradise.

Home—The place where we grumble the most and are treated the best.

Home—The center of our affections, round which our hearts best wishes twine.

Home—The place where our stomachs get three square meals daily and our hearts a thousand.

Home—The only place on earth where the faults and failings of humanity are hidden under the sweet mantle of charity.

(*Square and Compass*)

A TO Z

We should know every letter
  In our Craft's alphabet;
And some of them are better
  Then others are, and yet
Each one as an initial
  Some phase of brotherhood
May show as beneficial,
  And all of them are good.
If we would praise be earning,
  We'll let our brothers see
We have sufficient learning
  To go from A to Z.
Then let us all work harder,
  Show how we really feel.
Yes, let us start with Ardor,
  And let us end with Zeal.

(WOR. BRO. WALTER K. BELT, Newport, Oregon)

DON'T DO

Among the people of the Far East the Golden Rule is reversed. Instead of saying, "do unto others as you would have them do unto you" they express it, "*don't* do unto others what you would not have them do unto you."

There is much to be said for this interpretation. The things men *don't* do determine the kind of persons they are as surely as the things they *do* do. While there are many wonderful people doing good things there are countless others who are making a helpful contribution by not doing bad things. We may *not* like certain individuals, but it adds cubits to character if we keep our mouth shut about it. Each day brings inspiring opportunities to practice "don't do"—to the lasting benefit of many—ourselves included.

(*The Little Gazette*)

HOW TO GET ALONG WITH PEOPLE

Keep skid chains on your tongue; always say less than you think; cultivate a low persuasive voice.

Make promises sparingly and keep them faithfully, no matter what it costs you.

Praise good work done, regardless of who did it. If criticism is merited, criticize helpfully, never spitefully.

Preserve an open mind on all debatable questions. Discuss but don't argue. It is a mark of superior minds to disagree and yet be friendly.

(From *The Philalethes*)

"And another thing, I wish you wouldn't refer to my Masonic meetings as 'doing my thing'!"

II

"A man isn't poor if he can still laugh."
(HITCHCOCK)

HAPPY ENDING

Charges were preferred against Bro. J. . . . . . ., a member of Carl Junction Lodge No. 549 for un-Masonic conduct—in that while a guest of the Missouri Masonic Home, he had married a wife, another guest of the Home, all in violation of the rules of the institution, and to the scandal and disgrace of Freemasonry.

Trial was held resulting in his expulsion.

In due time an appeal was taken and the case is now before us for disposition.

It seems that from what we gather, that after Bro. J. . . . . . . hied himself, with his fair fiancée to Clayton, where the Hymeneal Knot was tied, he returned to the Home and imparted to the constitutional authorities what he had done. When lo, and behold, he was confronted with the startling statement that he and his bride could no longer remain in the home, and would have to seek quarters elsewhere. A good brother assisted in procuring employment for Bro. J., and things went along apparently well—well until his home lodge found out what he had done, when charges were preferred as above set forth, with the results indicated.

Does this interesting narrative end here? We trow not.

Shortly after the brother's expulsion, *his wife inherited $300,000.*

The committee went on to comment:

It is true the brother violated one of the rules of the Masonic Home in getting married, whether he knew it at the time he was violating it, we are not advised. But who are we to say that in doing so he was guilty of such un-Masonic conduct as would warrant the action taken by his lodge? We think not, for hath not marriage ever been regarded as an honorable institution?

Our first most excellent grand master, Solomon, King of Israel, hath said:

Who so findeth a wife, findeth a good thing, and obtaineth favor of the Lord.

This prophecy seems to have been abundantly realized in the case of Bro. J.

Again, we cannot see how the brother's offense could have operated to the detriment of the Home; after his marriage the Home was relieved of caring and providing for himself and wife. Cupid is no respecter of persons. His piercing arrows strike betimes where least suspected. Can we blame our brother?

Who travels alone without love on the heights
May laugh through the daytime,
But oft weeps through the night.
His courage goes down with the set of the sun
When the toils of life's journey
Are all borne by one.

We are informed that both Bro. J. and his wife are excellent people, though when the charges were preferred, they were in humble walks of life:

Let not ambition mock their useful toil,
Their homely joys and destiny obscure
Nor grandeur hear with disdainful smile
The short and simple annals of the poor.
Full many a gem of purest ray serene
The dark unfathomed caves of ocean bear,
Full many a flower is born to blush unseen,
And waste its sweetness on the desert air.

Not so with our brother. For while adversity marked the lengthening shadows athwart life's rugged pathway in former times, in the sunset of his life, fickle fortune at last smiled upon him, and we feel assured that he may be able, with the kindly offices of his helpmeet, to travel the remaining portion of his earthly pilgrimage in lolling luxury and unwonted uselessness.

Ill fares the land to hastening ills a Prey
Where wealth accumulates and men decay.

Let us not mar his coveted happiness by withholding our fraternal felicitations. We therefore recommend that the decision of the lodge be reversed, and that Bro. J. be restored to membership in his lodge. And may his tribe increase!

We do not know whether his tribe increased or not. We have our doubts. But at any rate, "all is well that ends well!"

(*Missouri Proceedings*)

"And, incidentally, the plural of Mason is Masons . . . not Masonites!"

A MASONIC SIGN

In 1930 an English ship on the way to Cuba was captured by a pirate vessel. The pirates looted the ship and were ready to burn it. In his distress, the English captain made the sign of E.A., to which one of the pirates answered with the sign of F.C. and interceded with his captain, who not only released the ship, but when he encountered it again, left it unmolested. On his return to England, the mate rushed to the nearest Masonic Lodge and applied for the degrees.

(*The New Age*)

FOOD FOR THOUGHT

If Masonry succeeds in bringing out the best in a man, it has served its purpose. A man is a Mason only when he is a man.

(*The Orange* (Mass.) *Masonic News Letter*)

HIS LAST RESORT

I just got back from Hankins' store,
And, from talk that's goin' round,
The Grand Master's a comin'
And no "Etiquette" can be found.

Our Master's goin' round and round,
Just like a great big top,
And if that "Etiquette" ain't found,
His heart will surely stop.

He's searched the Constitooshion,
And Proceedings, high and low,
But not a line has he ever found
To tell him how to go.

He's gone to Kuhn's "Centennial,"
Where Wisdom (condensed) is found,
But this "Sir Knight" on "Etiquette"
Has uttered not a sound.

But our Master's got a last resort,
If he has to go that far—
He'll hunt up the Worthy Matron
Of the local Eastern Star.

MASONIC RECIPE

Take 2 heaping cups PATIENCE
One heartful LOVE
2 handfuls GENEROSITY
Dash of LAUGHTER
One headful UNDERSTANDING
Sprinkle generously with KINDNESS
Add plenty of FAITH and mix well.
Spread over a period of a lifetime
and serve everybody you meet.

"I'm a little rusty on my Morse code but I think he's asking 'What lodge?'"

BUILDING STONE

A Boy is the only thing that God can use to make a Man and a Man is the only thing we can use to make a Mason.

(Grand Lodge of Missouri)

MASONIC BACKGROUND

In Iowa is a town which was orginally known as Shibboleth, later as Masonic Grove and later it became Mason City, Iowa. It was founded by Masons.

(*California Freemason*)

FREEMASONS, FROGS AND CENTIPEDES

A centipede was happy until a frog in fun said, "Pray which leg comes after which?"

This raised her mind to such a pitch, she lay distracted in the ditch, considering how to run.

I forgot where I first read this jinglet, but are not we Freemasons playing centipede? On every hand we hear the croaking of what ails Freemasonry, while we metaphorically lie distracted in the ditch of our own indolence.

Our troubles would pass away like clouds in a summer sky if we started living Freemasonry instead of talking about it. The charge to a newly-installed Master contains the essence of Masonic instruction:

"When a man is said to be a Freemason the world at large may know that he is one to whom the burdened heart may pour forth its sorrow, whose hand is guided by justice and whose heart is expanded by benevolence."

Let us get up out of the ditch and go to work. There's lots to be done.

(J. P. Myers, British Columbia—in the *California Freemason*)

HARMONIOUS FAITH

A district deputy grand master in 1897 reported that he had not visited any lodges in his district, but:

"that all is harmonious and prosperous,"

which prompted the grand master to remark:

"Harmony and prosperity are essentials, but existence of such conditions should be based, not on Faith, but on sight."

CHOP HIM DOWN TO SIZE, BOYS

Visiting a small country lodge in Vermont, the brother from a large lodge in Boston was listing the important men who belonged to his lodge. "Have any big men been born around here," he asked. "Nope, Brother," was the reply. "Best we can do is babies. Different in Boston, I reckon!"

STAR TREK

How far should charity extend?
We learn, where there is dearth,
Our charity should reach the end,
The utmost end of earth;
And even more. The arch of blue,
The great celestial sphere,
Should know the love of Masons, true,
That spreads fraternal cheer.
As astronauts in these days ride
To every stellar place,
So may we spread our teachings wide
Through all the realms of space.
(WALTER K. BELT, P.M.)

MINI-RESOLUTION

A century ago, and even later, it was the custom of lodges, when a brother died, to appoint a committee to draw up "memorial resolutions." These often occupied several pages of the lodge record. John D. Vincil, one-time grand secretary in Missouri, recorded this choice specimen which deserves mention for its brevity—if nothing else:

(a) Resolved, 1st: that Bro. .... is dead.
(b) Resolved: that we are sorry for it.

MASONIC LIBRARY

From an old library card coming into our (Grand Lodge of Iowa) possession, we learn that Cedar Rapids Masons were interested in a Masonic library long before the present library was ever dreamed of. The card is headed "Cedar Rapids Masonic Library, instituted January, 1859," and following the regulations pertaining to the loan of books is the title "Fines," one of which is,

that "for each leaf turned down there shall be paid five cents";

"for each leaf soiled ten cents";

"for a leaf torn or lost the borrower must pay the price of the book." . . . Evidently the Masons of Cedar Rapids were interested in Masonic literature at a pretty early date.

NO TICKEE—NO LAUNDLY

In 1875, the Master of Alton Lodge No. 255 (Missouri), removed the lodge charter to his home "to keep the lodge from working."

MASONIC PHILATELY

"I save Masonic Stamps" said Jones.

"What company gives them out?" Smith asked. "My wife saves Green Stamps and the Grand Union Stamps."

It's not funny, McGee, at least not to the 800 members of the Masonic Stamp Club of New York. They're a different breed of pups than I knew when I was a kid.

When I first started to save stamps, I saved everything from Albania to Zanzibar. My album was filled with stamps from each country. I didn't paste them in, I used hinges!

Now that I have graduated into senility, I find that I had a misspent youth, at least according to the Masonic collectors and philatelists. They do not place a value on quantity, they do not place a dollar sign on every stamp.

What binds these men together? Not the fact that they grant the degree Master of Philately. Not that they want to rub shoulders with Masters, Past Masters, Right Worshipfuls or Grand Masters. Not the fact that they want some place to go on the first Friday of each month. It is the acquisitive instinct, the master builder technique.

One collector saves envelopes with stamps affixed, each bearing a cancellation from a town having a special Masonic connection, or significance with Masonry. In his album are stamps bearing such cancellations as Three Points, Ashlar, Compass, Bible, Square.

Not one of these envelopes costs more than ten cents and a little time to acquire. To start a similar collection all you have to do is write a letter to the postmaster asking him to return the self-addressed stamped envelope to you. Your total cost, the cost of the postage to the specific post office, the cost of the postage for the return, plus the two envelopes, a short note requesting the cancellation and a little time and patience.

Another collector tries to obtain stamps from every state bearing the same cancellation. For example, his goal may be a stamped cancellation from Hiram, Alabama; Hiram, Alaska; Hiram, Arkansas, etc.

Another collector only saves stamps depicting famous Masons, while another saves only stamps on which Masonic regalia appears. Other collectors are more specific. They limit their collection to stamp depicting a specific Mason, such as Washington, Churchill, *et al.* Other collectors save only stamps and envelopes bearing Masonic cancellations. This is rather unusual today but was fairly common when each postmaster made up his own cancellation.

There is a large group of collectors who save envelopes which have been sent "free" and without stamps, a privilege given by the government to special individuals, such as the widows of Presidents, members of Congress, members of the armed forces, etc. The Masonic stamp collectors confine their efforts only to those bearing signatures by Masons.

Still another group of collectors save covers or envelopes bearing the names of towns and cities having the same names as those of distinguished Masons.

A little removed from philately, yet akin to it, is the collection of envelopes bearing in the lefthand corner the printed name of the sender. These collections are distinctive. One man saves only those envelopes from the Masonic Grand Lodges, another brother collects envelopes from every lodge in his state.

The assembling of these collections is not new to those members of the Masonic Stamp Club, but to me they were illuminating and interesting, and an excuse to stay home nights without looking at a 1925 movie. And for those who were not privileged to attend their meetings, I have briefly tried to explain their hobbies.

(WOR. JOSEPH N. KANE—in *The Empire State Mason*)

"All my aprons are at the cleaners."

YEA, VERILY

A zealous young Master was brought to task by the Grand Master for "jazzing up" the degree work with Bee-Bop music. To illustrate his point the Most Worshipful pointed out that "eager beavers are not necessarily the best dam builders."

THE LOST CHORD

One man gets nothing but discords from the keys of a piano; another gets harmony. No one claims the piano is at fault. Life is that same way. The discord is there; so is the harmony. Play it correctly and it gives forth the beauty; play it falsely and it will utter ugliness. But life is not at fault. The trouble lies in the player.

(From *The Freemason*)

NEARLY FINISHED

A visiting brother entered a lodge in the middle of the lecture on the third degree and seated himself in the rear of the room. After a while he began to fidget. Leaning over to an old brother at his side, evidently an old member of the lodge, he whispered:

"How long has he been lecturing?"

"Three or four years, I believe," the old brother answered.

"I'll stay then," said the visitor. "He must be nearly finished."

KEPT HIM POSTED

"Solomon, you know, was considered the wisest man on earth."

"Yes. His wives probably kept him informed concerning all that was going on."

RELIGION AND BUSINESS

"Parson," exclaimed Ephraim, "I've got religion - religion - I tell you."

"That's fine, brother. Now you are going to lay aside all sin?"

"Yes sir!"

"You're going to church?"

"Yes sir, yes sir!"

"You are going to care for the widows and orphans?"

"Oh, yes sir!"

"You are going to pay your debts?"

" Sir! that ain't religion; that's business!"

III

"From the sublime to the ridiculous there is but one step!"
(NAPOLEON)

OBJECTION

The Grand Master of Missouri gave a dispensation to reballot on a candidate. A brother entered objection, not on account of the unworthiness of the candidate, but because the Grand Master did not understand the law and the usages of the Fraternity—and to *discourage such ignorance,* objection was necessary.

WHAT A SIGHT!

A lodge paper in Kansas City in describing the program for the cornerstone laying of the Truman Library says:

The grand lodge will open at the Independence Masonic Temple, from where the procession will march to the sight (sic) of the ceremony.

And the procession proved to be a "sight" as it moved toward the "site."

SHORTEST CLOSING

A lodge in Massachusetts prided itself in always closing not later than 10:00 p.m. One night recently, though, the program was full, degree-work wasn't completed until 9:55.

Looking nervously at the clock, the Master announced that he was about to close the lodge. Rapping the gavel, he said, "Brother Senior Warden, are you a Master Mason?"

"I am," replied the Senior Warden.

"So am I," said the Master, "I now declare Charles W. Moore Lodge closed! Brother Senior Deacon attend at the altar." And the lodge was closed!

(*Editor's note:* While ritualists will question this story as to its legality, in several jurisdictions—Massachusetts being one—the ritual is regarded as "under the direction of the Master.")

"So then I told him, 'you'll have to choose between me and those stupid Masons!'"

ALL SHOOK UP

Another "short form" closing was recounted in an article (Winter 1968-1969, *The Royal Arch Mason*) written by Bro. John R. Nocas of California. It was at the annual convocation of the Grand Chapter of Royal Arch Masons of the State of California held during the terrible earthquake at San Francisco on April 18, 1906.

Although the temple had been shaken to its foundations by the repeated shocks, and in spite of warnings that the building was unsafe, they convened for their election and installation. Ten tremors were counted during their rapid conduct of business. As they were about to close, someone shouted, "Get out of here, every mother's son of you, as quick as God will let you, or you'll be crushed in a minute."

Brother Nocas commented, "The grand chapter was then closed in probably the shortest form ever and the nervous companions hastened from the doomed structure." He concluded his article with this observation. "Probably the only humorous aspect of the convocation, and this in retrospect, was that for the first and only time in California Grand Chapter history none of the delegates waited around for their traveling expenses.

"That night the temple was in ashes."

PETTICOAT MASON

A brother we know finally succumbed to the "wishes" of his wife and submitted his petition to the Eastern Star. He received the usual kidding about becoming a "petticoat Mason" and the usual taunts about what he would have to go through in his initiation. He was pleasantly surprised to find that the initiation was one of impressive dignity. At the refreshment hour following the degree-work, when called upon for a few words, he related his experience. He said that he really hadn't taken any of the kidding seriously until that night when getting ready to come to chapter, his "dear wife," in all seriousness had insisted that he wear lace-trimmed bloomers. Our hero then expressed disappointment that no one had asked to see if he was "properly prepared" and forthwith dropped his pants, exposing bright lavender bloomers, trimmed in yards of lace.

"THOSE ARE MY PEOPLE"

When Bro. Vinton Hayworth was a guest on the Jack Paar Show in 1960, he was asked how well he knew Cliff Arquette (Charley Weaver). Hayworth replied that he knew him well enough to propose him for membership and signed his Masonic petition. (They are members of Ravenswood Lodge No. 777 of Chicago.)

LINES TO THE STEWARDS

In one of the American-Canadian lodges in Germany, the Stewards prepared and served the refreshments after every meeting. It was always the same thing—hot dogs—which caused one brother with a delicate digestive system to pose the question if a change of menu couldn't be arranged. He got his point across by addressing these lines to the Stewards:

Sometimes I think it almost lewd
To call the stuff you serve us food.

ON WHEELS

R.W. Reginald F. Berry of Maine furnishes us with the following item:

On November 11, 1964, a special communication of the Grand Lodge of Kansas was held aboard a moving railway train, in two special cars attached to "The Chief," one of the crack trains of the Santa Fe system. This unique meeting was held to honor "the many distinguished Masons who have been and still are active in the railroading business." Special mention was made of Cyrus K. Holliday, Deputy Grand Master of the Grand Lodge of Kansas from 1861 to 1866, the founder of the Santa Fe Railway and one of the founders of the City of Topeka. Numerous present-day railroad men participated in this meeting, the principal address being delivered by Bro. Jack E. Lester, retired Assistant General Manager of the Santa Fe. So far as we know, this is the only time that a Grand Lodge has actually met "on wheels."

(*The Wayfarer*—1965)

LIMITED KNOWLEDGE

At a gathering of women the conversation turned to a discussion of Masons. Some of the women seemed to be rather well informed on the subject, and discussed it at some length, but one woman was bored and finally remarked, "Well, I don't know much about Masons, but I think their fruit jars are very nice."

SECRETARY'S NOTE

Forget the hasty, unkind word;
Forget the slander you have heard;
Forget the quarrel and the cause;
Forget the whole affair, because,
Forgetting is the only way.
Forget the storm of yesterday.
Forget the knocker, and the squeak;
Forget the bad day of the week.
Forget you're not a millionaire;
Forget the grey streaks in your hair;
Forget to even get the blues—
But Don't Forget
To Pay your Dues!

(*Eric Scottish Rite News*)

GOING UP

"Everything is going up!" Well, the rain's still coming down; there's no tax on sunshine, or the red and gold and brown of autumn leaves, or on the snow that makes a mountain crown.

"Everything is going up!" But bird songs cost no more; no 20 per cent for luxury on the jasmine around the door; and moonlight in my garden's inexpensive as before.

"Everything is going up!" But the price of joy's the same; it costs no more to work or sing, or fan the ancient flame of love; and to a comrade's smile we still may stake our claim.

"Everything is going up!" Come, come, what's that you say? The things that really matter cost just the same today. The broad blue sea, the mountain tops, the trees, the rain, the sky; they're tax exempt forever—oh lucky you and I.

(*Scottish Rite Torch*)

"Just tell him we met at the last Convocation—he'll know who it is."

GREETED WITH BRASS BAND

An article in the Chicago *Daily News* tells of the work being done by a Chicago engineer in Italy; the article says:

Arenberg struck up a working agreement with *Publio Cortini,* an Italian lighting engineer, who knows American lighting.

Cortini has a warm spot for Chicago because as Grand Master of the Masons in Italy he was welcomed with a brass band in Chicago.

10 KEYS TO "BETTER BROTHERHOOD"

Speak to your Brothers. There is nothing as heart-warming as a cheerful word of greeting.

Smile. It takes 72 muscles to frown—only 14 to smile.

Call your Brothers by name. The sweetest music to anyone's ears is the sound of his own name.

Be friendly. If you would have friends you must be friendly.

Be cordial. Speak and act as if everything you do were a genuine pleasure.

Be interested in people. You can like everybody if you try.

Be generous with praise—cautious with criticism. Be considerate of the feelings of others. It will be appreciated.

Be thoughtful of the opinions of others. There are three sides to a controversy—yours, the other fellow's, and the right one.

Be ever ready to serve. What counts most in life is what we do for others.

(Valley of Trenton)

AIR POLLUTION

Three Grand Masters recently met during the annual communication of one of the western Grand Lodges; they were Howell (Howl), Bray, and Holleran (Hollerin). Noisy outfit we should say?

AUNT MINNIE'S AUTOMOBILE

Years ago Aunt Minnie decided that it was time she owned an automobile. Very few families had them then, especially maiden ladies, but one friend after another joined the ranks of motorists until it was more than she could stand.

When she went to the weekly meeting of the sewing circle she was left completely out of the conversation. Now the talk was about horsepower where once it was about flower gardens and pies. At the Ladies Aid Society there was some mention of the Bible, foreign missions, and the preacher's wife, but there was more and more talk about miles per gallon or how to repair a puncture. So Aunt Minnie bought one. She went to the dealer and said, "I'll take that one," wrote a check for the full amount and told him to deliver it the following week. She then went to a contractor to order a garage built to house the automobile.

The garage was built and the new automobile was delivered. The salesman informed her that he was ready to give her some driving lessons. That day was not convenient for the first lesson so she asked him to drive the automobile into the garage and promised to let him know when it would be convenient for her to begin driving.

Day after day passed without Aunt Minnie calling the salesman. Weeks rolled by and so did months. At the end of the year she bought a new license but never got around to taking her first driving lesson. Years passed and at the beginning of each one she bought a new license but never moved the car. This continued until the day she died.

Poor old Aunt Minnie never realized the pleasures she missed. The automobile was paid for. The streets were there and she helped to pay for them, too, but the automobile remained in the garage.

The only pleasure she obtained from the automobile was in her ability to tell her friends she owned it.

Aunt Minnie was a screwball, but don't be too hard on her until after you have looked in the mirror. Did you write a check for your Masonic initiation fees as Aunt Minnie wrote one for her automobile? Did you take the Degrees just as Aunt Minnie had a garage built? Do you pay your dues each year just as she bought the license for her automobile? Do you let your membership sit in the garage and rust like that automobile? If you do . . . Hi!—Aunt Minnie.

(*The California Freemason*)

MATT DILLON'S WATERING PLACE

We have been informed that the real owner of the "Long Branch Saloon" in Dodge City, Kansas, in 1874, was C. M. "Chalk" Beeson, a Freemason who served as a state representative and was sheriff of Ford County in 1892. Perhaps he hired "Kitty" as a front?

(*The Royal Arch Mason*—Fall 1968)

PRETTY SOFT

We recently heard a Junior Warden described as "the *pillow* of Beauty."

DOWN UNDER

In a dinner which followed the annual convocation of the Supreme Grand Chapter of Scotland, the proceedings record the following bit of humor:

Companion Lyons spoke of the great pleasure it gave him to present the greetings of his Companions in New South Wales. He was a Glasgow man exalted in Australia and in Australia they did not hold it against him that he was a Scot. Australians said there were two pests in their country, rabbits and Scotsmen. They had myxomatosis to help them to get rid of the rabbits but nothing for Scotsmen! (Loud laughter.)

"TINY BUBBLES IN THE WINE"

The liquor situation still appears in proceedings of Grand Lodges. In some states there seems to be a lessening of restrictions on sales by members, while in other jurisdictions the laws seem to be tightening.

An amusing incident is reported from Georgia, where a brother was tried for engaging in the sale of liquor. His attorney, who appeared to be a Freemason, wrote a letter to the lodge, in which the trial was held, calling the Grand Officers and others, "bubbleheads," which did not improve the situation when it got to the Grand Lodge. The actual statement was:

"We cannot allow the Women's Christian Temperance Union, acting by and through bubbleheads, to do, by indirect means, what they cannot accomplish directly."

The writer of the letter was tried by his own lodge, and the lodge reported it had one less "bubblehead" when the trial was completed.

PANTY RAID

While on the subject of trials, one of the trial reports in the Grand Lodge *Proceedings of California* tells of a certain brother who had been convicted for the selling of certain goods which included 181 pairs of ladies Argo Knit pants. In making its report, the committee said:

"We do not wish to be misunderstood as overemphasizing the gravity of that specification against the accused in which he is charged with a 'panty raid.' Indulgence in such conduct by boys of college age for the purpose of displaying either skill or courage, if that be the purpose, differs somewhat from the conduct of the accused here, in that the theft of 181 pairs of ladies pants is not merely a playful prank."

WELCOME TO SANTA FE

The Master of Santa Fe, New Mexico, Lodge was quite humorous in extending a welcome to the Grand Lodge. He informed the Grand Lodge that the proper dress for all formal occasions was a Western shirt, bolo tie, levis and cowboy boots. To shave or not is optional, but a haircut will immediately establish you as a "furriner." They were asked not to make derogatory remarks about their architecture. A short length of rope hanging from one of the cottonwoods in the plaza was all that remained to the memory of a certain Mr. Gable. If occasion became necessary to ride one of the city buses, they should not do so without adequate provision, for a stranger a week previous had boarded a bus marked "Aqua Fria" and wound up three days later in Ojo Caliente. In conclusion, they were notified if they got into difficulties with the police they should not call the mayor, for it would serve no useful purpose and might get them an additional 30 days.

THINK MINK

A brother we know who is active in every Masonic body in town bought his wife a mink stole. One of his friends remarked that it was a beautiful piece of fur and should keep her warm. To which our friend replied, "I didn't buy it to keep her WARM; I bought it to keep her QUIET. She's always yakking about being a Masonic Widow."

"I've been a Mason for years, but this is the first time I knew we had a Temple."

INITIATION

Long years ago, I climbed a stair
   And rapped at an ancient door.
I passed within a temple fair
   And trod the checkered floor.

I passed between the pillars two;
   I climbed the winding stair;
The letter "G" then met my view;
   I earned my wages there.

I knelt beside the altar fair
   I counted not the cost.
I searched afar with earnest care,
   But still the *W*ord was lost.

Though some may think my search absurd,
   When time shall ebb and fail,
I hope to learn the final *W*ord
   Beyond life's mystic veil.

(D. C. TIDWELL, P.M., Texas—
The Texas Freemason, August 1967)

GO TO HELL!

Lloyd Wilson, Grand Secretary of California, quotes a Past Grand Master of Idaho as defining a diplomat—"a man who could tell you to go to hell in such nice language that you really look forward to the trip."

Along the same lines is the definition of *tact*—"the ability to tell a person to go to hell in such a way that he'll ask for a road map."

Speaking of *tact, TACT* (The American-Canadian Trestleboard) is the name of the fine publication of the American-Canadian Provincial Grand Lodge of the United Grand Lodges of Germany, Brotherhood of German Freemasons.

And speaking of hell, that's what most of us catch from our wives when our Masonic meetings are too frequent, too long or too late.

But then, we should never be too critical of our wives' judgement —look who they married.

ATTITUDE

To illustrate the relationship of our attitude toward Masonry, Masonic speakers frequently use variations of the story about the minister who was congratulating an actor upon his beautiful rendition of the Twenty-Third Psalm.

The actor replied, "Yes, Reverend, I know the Psalm, but you know the Shepherd."

CHANGING CIRCUMSTANCES

Another favorite which deals with attitudes is the story of the mountaineer who drove over to get a doctor. "I want you to see what you can do for my son-in-law. He's in bad shape," the mountaineer explained.

The doctor climbed into his wagon and accompanied the fellow to his home and found that it was no exaggeration that the son-in-law was in bad shape. He was really beaten up good. The mountaineer explained that they had been in a fight and he had worked over the youth. "Aren't you ashamed," exclaimed the doctor, "to beat your own son-in-law like that?" "Wal," drawled the mountaineer, "he waren't my son-in-law then."

. . . TO FIT THE CRIME

A well known brother and orator in British Columbia has the very symbolic and expressive initials G. A. B. (Gab).

CALLING THE SHOTS

M.W. Bro. Wallace Campbell, PGM of Maine, tells this story: "The first year that I was Grand Master, I attended the 100th anniversary joint celebration of Greenleaf and Drummond lodges. Sherm Parsons from New Hampshire was there and was received in my suite. When he was introduced, mention was made of the fact that he was 102 years of age. I had just had my 51st birthday and whispered to M.W. Bro. Paul Powers, 'Sherm is just twice as old as I am.' Brother Powers, who is well known for speaking his mind, replied, 'Yes, and he's twice the man you are.' "

I AM A MASON

"I am a Mason," said one flashing an expensive ring and twirling a charm on his vest.

"What makes you a Mason?" asked a humble Blue Lodge brother.

"Why, I have taken all the degrees I know of," said the former.

"How may I know you to be a Mason?" asked the humble brother.

"By this $100 ring and charm," was the honest answer.

A POLITICAL PARTY

A young lady reporter on a country paper was sent out to interview leading citizens as to their political leanings. "May I see the gentleman of the house?" she asked of a large woman who answered the doorbell.

"No, you can't!" was the decisive reply.

"But I only want to know to what party he belongs."

"Well, take a good look at me," was the stern reply, "I'm the party he belongs to."

TIT FOR TAT

Wife: "I have made up my mind, John, that when I married you, I married a fool."

Husband: "That reminds me of a remark you made just before we were married. You remember you said it would be hard to find two people more alike."

IV

"If a straw can tickle a man, it is an instrument of happiness."

(DRYDEN)

MASONRY BY EXAMPLE

Many Masonic speakers have used the following newspaper article to illustrate the necessity for us to "practice out of the lodge, those great moral duties inculcated in it."

EVERYBODY DOES IT!

When Johnny was six years old, he was with his father when they were caught speeding. His father handed the officer a $5 bill with his driver's license. "It's O.K., son," his father said as they drove off. "Everybody does it."

When he was nine, his mother took him to his first theater production. The box office man couldn't find any seats until his mother discovered an extra $2 in her purse. "It's O.K., son," she said. "Everybody does it."

When he was 12, he broke his glasses on the way to school. His Aunt Francine persuaded the insurance company that they had been stolen and they collected $27. "It's O.K.," she said. "Everybody does it."

When he was 15, he made right guard on the high school football team. His coach showed him how to block and at the same time grab the opposing end by the shirt so the official couldn't see it. "It's O.K., kid," the coach said. "Everybody does it."

When he was 16, he took his first summer job at the big market. His assignment was to put the over-ripe tomatoes in the bottom of the boxes and the good ones on top where they would show. "It's O.K., kid," the manager said. "Everybody does it."

When he was 18, Johnny and a neighbor applied for a college scholarship. Johnny was a marginal student. His neighbor was in the upper 3 per cent of his class, but he couldn't play right guard. Johnny got the assignment. "It's O.K.," they told him. "Everybody does it."

When he was 19, he was approached by an upperclassman who

offered the test answers for $3. "It's O.K., kid," he said. "Everybody does it." Johnny was caught and sent home in disgrace. "How could you do this to your mother and me?" his father said. "You never learned anything like this at home." His aunt and uncle were also shocked.

If there's one thing the adult world can't stand, it's a kid who cheats. . . .

(JACK GRIFFIN—*The Chicago Sun-Times*)

LETTER TO THE EDITOR

The Texas Freemason published by the Grand Lodge of Texas, in our opinion, is one of the finest Masonic publications. In the July 1967 issue under a heading, "A Member's Speak Special," we found this poignant letter.

Dear TTF:

In 1929 and '30, I was a patient in William Beaumont Army Hospital in El Paso. I belonged to an Illinois Lodge, but I had not paid my dues for some time. While in the hospital, I received a letter from the lodge. It said the lodge was building a new building; dues were being doubled; I would be dropped from the rolls if I did not pay my dues.

A Masonic Brother, Ben Harrison of Athens, Texas, lay in the bed next to mine. I read him the letter and commented, "I'm not going to pay those dues. Masonry hasn't done me any good and I don't have the money."

Ben replied, "Oh, I'd pay them if I were you." Then he told me a story.

Ben had been wounded in France and described what happened when he awoke in a hospital. "A doctor was bending over me," Ben related, "and I heard him say, 'He can't stand it now, but if he is still alive in the morning, we'll amputate the leg.' Well, the next morning I was alive and awake. When the doctor came, I took a chance and identified myself as a Mason. I pleaded with him to save my leg. 'Brother,' he said, 'I will do everything in my power to save it, and if it is ever cut off, someone else will do it.' "

Ben then turned back the sheet and raised his scarred leg. "I still have my leg, thanks to Masonry! It's not as good as it used to be, but it is better than a wooden one!"

I paid my dues.

EDWIN S. BURTIS
Fraternity Lodge 111, El Paso

LARGEST, SMALLEST, AVERAGE

The following article also appeared in *The Texas Freemason,* December 1967, and is reprinted with permission.

Freemasonry is noted for the fact that it is truly universal. It welcomes members from all walks of life, from all religious denominations which acknowledge a Supreme Being and from all political persuasions.

Truly, Masons are an excellent cross-section of life.

During Grand Lodge, *TTF* thought it might be fun to take a look at these men who are Masons, so we found the largest, the smallest and a group which could easily be the average Masons in attendance at Grand Lodge.

The *TTF* camera searched out Bro. Ray C. Stevenson, Master of John Sayles Lodge 1403 in Abilene, who was obviously the largest Mason in Waco, and posed him with Bro. John S. Clifton of Austin Lodge 12, who, at 48 inches of height, was easily the smallest Mason to be found in the Grand Lodge Temple.

Then, *TTF* rounded up an average age group of Masons from one lodge. These Brethren all came to Grand Lodge from Harlingen Lodge 1132 and averaging some facts about them provides a typical picture of average Masons from Texas Lodges.

These ten Brethren represent a total of 132 years of Masonry. One is currently Master of his lodge. Three are Past Masters and one is a newly-appointed District Deputy Grand Master. The youngest member of the Fraternity has been a Mason for three years and the oldest has served Masonry 27 years.

As a group, they have traveled a total of some 22,400 miles in their Masonic activities. Four of the ten hold Certificates from the Committee on Work of the Grand Lodge of Texas.

They average 46 years of age, with the youngest being 36 and the eldest chalking up 65 years. Together, they have sired 23 children and are proud grandparents of five. They have been married for an average of over 23 years and served a total of over 57 years in the armed forces for their country.

Not a bad average for just a typical group of ten Masons at Grand Lodge, is it?

It was fun to prove that Masons are, in fact, an admirable cross-section of life!!

HEAP BIG BROTHER!

In the February 5, 1851 issue of *Odd Fellow,* we came upon this interesting bit of information: "TECUMSEH was a Mason—a terrible warrior, but we must remember, he fought for his oppressed country. At the battle of the river RAISIN, he rescued several pale-faces from destruction, on finding they were Brothers."

"Denton, wouldn't you be happier as an Elk, or perhaps a Moose?"

AND THERE WAS LIGHT

From the transactions of the Quator Coronati Lodge of Research in Ireland, we have selected the following bit of Irish humor:

Among the items purchased by an Irish Lodge in 1818 are the following:

Powder and nitre	005
Do. and flint	003
Weir (Wire)	004½

What were they used for?

The answer is told by an Irish historian who says that when searching in a rural Masonic hall for the vanished archives of a certain old lodge, he found a piece of wood, rudely shaped like the grip of a pistol, but with no mechanism attached. The front part had a hollow groove as though to receive the barrel of a pistol. In answer to the question:

What on earth was this used for?

The local veteran said:

I thou(gh)t thot ould thing was burnt long ago. I'll tell you what thot ould thing was used for. A child's wee cannon was put in thon hollow and tied on wi' a bit of wire. Well, in the ould days, they filled the wee cannon with gun-powther, and put a wee drappie powther in the wee touch-hole; and do ye min' thon time when God said let there be light—well, they put a lit match to thon wee hole —and then—mind ye—when thon wee thing was let off—there WAS light.

FACULTY OF TACITURNITY

We are indebted to the pages of *The Freemasons' Monthly Magazine,* April 1851, for this quotation of Rev. Brother Oliver who "satirizes the inquisitiveness of the uninitiated, in respect to the peculiar features and observances of the Masonic Brotherhood":

"What is Masonry? This is a great and important question which has puzzled the heads of all the uninitiated from the day of its first establishment to our own most peculiar times. What is Masonry? I could give 50 definitions of it if I chose to be communicative; but I should consider myself 'Courteous overmuch' were I to furnish the cowan with too great a portion of information at once. He would be gorged into a plethoric habit of mind, which would set him cackling like a young pullet after she had laid her first egg, and hops around the farmyard in an ecstacy of joy to tell her companions what a feat she has done. I shall give him only one definition at present, and he may muse on it at his leisure. Freemasonry is a triangle upon a triangle, placed in the centre towards the rising of the sun; chequered with the *opus Grecanicum,* circumscribed with the scroll work, permeating through the sephiroth, and graduating to a perfect heptad! There! Let the cowan digest that, and I will then impart some further instruction to edify his mind."

"Our guest speaker tonight doesn't need any introduction because he didn't show up."

SLAP

A brother from Missouri Lodge No. 1, in 1901, was acquitted by his lodge on the charge of slapping his wife "to keep her from stealing his money." The grand lodge did not agree with the decision of the lodge—since which time it has been dangerous, *in Missouri,* to slap one's wife.

COMMERCIAL ENTERPRIZE

The Wisconsin proceedings record the fact that a brother desired authority to have a group of Job's Daughters use the following statement on printed cards:

"Baby Sitters Bureau
for Masonic families"

It was ruled that the word "Masonic" was being used for commercial gain by individuals or outside organizations.

MR. FIXIT FINDS IT

The Philadelphia Evening Bulletin carries a column by "Mr. Fixit" who helps readers solve a myriad of problems. Last February 21 this letter appeared in the column: "I have been searching, without success, for a set of snooker balls. I want to send them to a friend who operates a restaurant in Rome. He flies to Malta once a month to attend a meeting of his Masonic Lodge. There is a pool table in one of the lodge rooms. Many years ago a British company gave the lodge a set of snooker balls, but these have become worn and should be replaced. My friend has searched all over Europe for replacements. When he failed to find them over there, he asked me to look for a set in the United States." Incidentally, "Mr. Fixit" found them!

(*The Royal Arch Mason*—Fall 1968)

COWANS, EAVESDROPPERS AND . . .

The Tiler was getting more than his share of harassment from the brethren prior to the opening. The smoke-filled anteroom was crowded. The banter was jovial. But, as usual, there was one brother who sensed he was getting the Tiler's "goat," so he continued with his jibes.

Finally, the Tiler stopped him with, "My job is to keep off cowans and eavesdroppers. I wish it also included keeping off *troublemakers."*

SQUARE

An old brass square was found under the foundation stone of an old bridge in Limerick, Ireland in 1830. The inscription upon the square was dated 1517:

"I will strive to live,
With love and care,
Upon the level
By the square."

MISINFORMATION

Time magazine's reportorial staff may have erred, or it may have been prompted to say in the issue of July 31, 1964 that "the Order of the Shrine is no frivolous minor offshoot but the *second highest level* of all Masonry." (I have been wondering ever since what the *top level* of Masonry is considered to be. You can bet your bottom dollar that it is not the Ancient Craft Lodge.)

(M.W. Dwight L. Smith—Indiana)

FATHER AND SON

Raisings of sons by fathers are quite common. And there have been many instances of sons raising their fathers. The *Proceedings of the Grand Lodge of China* record that on July 1, 1967, Wor. Bro. C. H. Chang installed his son as Master of Sun Lodge No. 6, in Taipei. Wor. Bro. Raymond Chang, in turn, installed his father as Secretary of Sun Lodge.

VIRGINITY—UNHEARD OF

The Grand Master of Delaware told the Grand Lodge of Virginia that the headmaster in one of the Virginia schools asked one of the boys in his class to read the opening scripture lesson. The boy turned to the St. Matthew parable of the ten virgins and read: "Behold, ten Virginians went out to meet the bridegroom; five of them were wise and five were foolish." The headmaster said, "Read that again"; and he said, "Behold, there were ten Virginians went forth to meet the bridegroom; five of them were wise and five were foolish." The headmaster thought a few minutes, and said, "Well, if it's in the Bible it must be true, but I cannot conceive of five foolish Virginians."

A QUESTION OF DOROTHY DIX

In one of Dorothy's columns which gives advice on everything from birth to death, a "perplexed wife" (most of them are) asks:

My husband and I have always been close to each other and never kept anything from each other until recently when he joined the Mason's Lodge. He has taken his first degree and will not tell me anything about what goes on. Everything is secret and it is eating my heart out.

Instead of advising the perplexed wife to go join the Star, she replies:

Where have you been all your life that you have not known that every man who joins the Masonic Lodge takes a solemn oath (obligation?) not to reveal the secrets of the organization? If he went about discussing what occurred at their meetings he would forfeit the respect of all decent men. Instead of nagging your husband about what goes on at the meetings, be satisfied to know that he belongs to one of the noblest and most altruistic organizations in the world.

Bully for Dorothy!

HERE COME DE JUDGE

When Judge Walter Dickie Allen was Master of Athelstan Lodge (in Worcester, and incidentally, the largest Lodge in Massachusetts), one of the duties of the Inside Sentinel at that lodge was to place a glass of water on the podium. The Inside Sentinel, being of a frivolous nature and thinking he could have some fun, placed a glass of gin on the podium. Everyone but the Master knew what was in the glass. During the Master's ritual, he became thirsty and reached for the glass. But, instead of looking perplexed and knowing that liquor of any kind was taboo in any lodge, he guzzled down the entire glass of gin without even batting an eyelash. He did not even ask any questions or chastise anyone. He felt refreshed and continued on with the work of the evening being none the worse off for it all. The membership of the lodge was greatly upset for fear that the Master might become inebriated . . . but no such luck. The Judge was unaffected in any way, and according to his version, his ritual was just as bad as ever. But the work went on for the evening and the Master was "as sober as a Judge."

V

"Wit is the salt of conversation, not the food."
(HAZLITT)

THE LETTER "E"

Someone has advanced the opinion that the letter "E" is the most unfortunate character in the English alphabet, because it is always out of cash, forever in debt, never out of danger, in hell all the time, and has never been in Indiana, Ohio, or Masonry.

But we call his attention to the fact that "E" has doubled up in Freemasonry and is never in war and always in peace. It is the beginning of existence, the commencement of ease and the end of trouble.

Without it there would be no meat, no life, no Heaven. It is in the center of honesty, makes love perfect and without it there would be no editors and no news.

WELL SAID

One of the greatest inspirations of Masonry is to sit in a lodge room and look around at the older men present; men with the snow of many winters in their hair and the weight of a long and useful life bearing down upon the once stalwart shoulders.

In their faces, as they attentively watch the work or listen to the lectures or discussions, you always see genuine interest, close attention, calmness, confidence in the principles exemplified. Month after month for many years—30, 40, a hoary half-century—they have come through fair weather and foul. They have come sometimes many miles to listen to these truths and to present them to younger Brethren. You see them today. Could you have been there, you would have seen others several hundred years ago.

This enduring appeal of Masonry; this wisdom in its lessons that fit the needs of all ages and generations; this lifelong loyalty seen in the lives of so many patriarchs in every community, is one of the best proofs that through a human organization, Masonry is a purposeful instrument of Divine Hands.

(*Masonry at Work*—June, 1969)

AMEN, PASTOR

Presiding officers of various bodies find this "parable" useful in their pep talks:

A negro pastor was working on his congregation. He said, "This church has been sitting down on the job, but it's going to get up and walk." A deacon said, "Amen, pastor! Make 'er walk!" And the preacher said, "It's going to do more than walk—it's going to get up and run!" And the deacon said, "Amen, pastor! Make 'er run!" The preacher said, "It's going to get up and fly!" And the deacon said, "Amen! Hallelujah! Make 'er fly!" And the preacher leaned over the pulpit and said, "But brothers and sisters, it's going to cost money to make this church fly." And the deacon said, "Let 'er walk, brother, let 'er walk!"

FOR FRIENDS OF THE AGED

Blessed are they who understand
my faltering step and palsied hand.

Blessed are they who know that my ears today
must strain to catch the things they say.

Blessed are they who seem to know
that my eyes are dim and my wits are slow.

Blessed are they who looked away
when coffee spilled at table today.

Blessed are they with a cheery smile
who stop to chat for a little while.

Blessed are they who never say
"You've told that story twice today."

Blessed are they who make it known
that I'm loved, respected and not alone.

Blessed are they who know the ways
to bring back memories of yesterday.

Blessed are they who know I'm at a loss
to find the strength to carry the Cross.

Blessed are they who ease the days
on my journey Home in loving ways.

(Arlie H. Cook—Superintendent Masonic Home Grand Lodge of Alabama)

"I knew Harry wouldn't miss the Convocation!"

LET US PRAY

At an installation of officers of Heidelberg Chapter No. 304, National Sojourners, Bro. (Maj. Gen.) Floyd Wergelund, who was then National President of National Sojourners, Inc., was the Installing Officer. The program was under way. There was a large group of Sojourners and their ladies present.

Suddenly, as it was time for the opening prayer, the Chapter President realized that the Chaplain was not present. He thrust a ritual into the hands of Wor. Bro. Benson Lennie, Master of Triangle Lodge No. 834, who was seated next to him, with the whispered request to read the prayer.

Wor. Brother Lennie impressively read the prayer which had been handed to him. It was the Funeral Prayer.

ALAS! POOR HIRAM!

Where the Hiramic Legend really came from no one knows. Hiram is mentioned in the Bible in I Kings and II Chronicles, stories written 700 years apart. He was also mentioned in the Cooke Ms. of 1410. But the Graham Ms., discovered in 1936 and dated 1726, and filled with Masonic ritual, tells the legend of Noah, which any Mason should find extremely interesting. The manuscript story is that a valuable secret died with Noah. His three sons, Shem, Ham, and Japheth, desirous of finding this secret, which they supposed Noah had carried with him into the grave, determined to exhume the body, "agreeing beforehand that if they did not find the very thing itself, the first thing they found was to be to them as a secret. They found nothing in the grave except the dead body; when the finger was gripped it came away, and so with the wrist and the elbow. They then reared up the dead body, supporting it by setting foot to foot, knee to knee, breast to breast, cheek to cheek and hand to back. One said here is yet marrow in this bone and the second said but a dry bone and the third said it stinketh."

("Masonry's Modern Mystery: The Origin of Its Ritual,"
Grand Oration by R.W. Louis L. Williams,
Grand Lodge of Illinois—1967)

DIGBY O'DELL, THE FRIENDLY . . .

William Loucks, past master of Beacon Lodge No. 3, St. Louis, Missouri, broke into the news in the *St. Louis Globe* recently, for while conducting an installation ceremony, he said to the new master, Calvin Feutz:

"Cal, I know people are dying to meet you."

The audience laughed, knowing that "Cal" was an undertaker.

TRANSLATED FROM CHINESE

The Monthly Summons of Amity Lodge No. 1 of the Grand Lodge of China bears this quotation of the Chinese Sage, Mencius (472-289 B.C.):

"As Square and Compass perfect and circles line, model of human kinship's best, the Saint doth shine."

WELCOMING BAND

Most Puissant General Grand Master George Verbryck in his address to the twenty-eighth Triennial Assembly of the General Grand Council of Royal and Select Masters told of his arrival at Sheridan, Wyoming, to attend the Grand Bodies there.

As he looked out of the plane, he was stunned to see a large crowd, a brass band, and flags waving. Smiling broadly and waving to the crowd upon leaving the plane, he found the grand welcome was not for him—but was for Miss Wyoming who was returning from the Miss Universe contest in the East.

ON PURPOSE?

"What do you mean insulting me in that yellow sheet of yours?" roared the politician at the editor.

"Now, just a minute," cautioned the editor, "Didn't we print that item exactly as you gave it to us, to the effect that you'd resigned as city treasurer?"

"You printed it correctly enough," conceded the grafter, then bellowed, "but look where you put it—in the column headed 'Public Improvements.' "

(*Oklahoma Mason*)

"Charles, having the lead in your high school senior play hardly qualifies you for the 'Freemasons in the Entertainment World' page."

MASONIC DANCE

Although it may sound like a revised version of the tired, old joke about how he got the black eye ("I thought he said 'stand up *and* shut up' "), a friend of ours claims the following incident actually happened in Scotia, New York.

The Senior Warden was instructing the candidate how to approach the East, when the candidate started hopping around on his left foot. When later asked what he thought the Senior Warden had said, the candidate replied, "I thought he said to 'dance.' "

THEY HADN'T SEEN EVERYTHING

In the *Scottish Year Book* (1956), under the heading: "Now We've Heard Everything," is quoted from the Connecticut proceedings a "decision by the Grand Master that a lodge may not charge admission to witness degree work."

HE COULD NOT HELP

Reading proceedings of grand lodges and grand chapters is not all dull reading as might be supposed. Royal Copeland, of Massachusetts, speaking before the Grand Chapter of Virginia told this:

I was traveling on the train across the country when the door of the Pullman opened and an agitated man called out:

"Is there a Catholic priest in the car?"

No one paid any attention and he went along to the next car

making the same inquiry. Nothing happened, and about ten minutes later he came back, opened the door of the car and asked:

"Is there an Episcopalian rector in the car?"

He returned a few minutes later looking rather dejected when a quiet little man arose and said:

"My good man, I heard you ask for a Catholic priest, and I heard you come back and ask for an Episcopalian rector. I happen to be a Baptist minister, and I wonder if I can be of any assistance to you?"

"Hell no," said the man, *"I was only looking for a corkscrew!"*

DAS VERGISSMEINNICHT—THE FORGET-ME-NOT

As early as the year 1934, soon after Hitler's rise to power, it became apparent Freemasonry was in danger. In the same year, the German Grand Lodge of the Sun in Beyreuth (one of the pre-war German Grand Lodges), realized the imminent problems facing them and elected to wear a little blue flower, the Forget-Me-Not, in lieu of the traditional Square and Compasses, as a mark of identity for Masons. It was felt the new symbol would not attract attention from the Nazis, who were in the process of confiscating and appropriating Masonic Lodges and property. Masonry had gone underground and it was necessary that the Brethren have some readily recognizable means of identification.

Throughout the entire Nazi era, a little blue flower in the lapel marked a Brother. In the Concentration Camps and in the cities a little blue Forget-Me-Not distinguished the lapels of those who refused to allow the light of Masonry to be extinguished.

In 1947, when the Grand Lodge of the Sun was reopened in Bayreuth by Past Grand Master Beyer, a little blue pin, in the shape of a Forget-Me-Not, was proposed and adopted as the official emblem of the first annual convention of those who survived the bitter years of semi-darkness, bringing the Light of Masonry once again into the Temples.

At the Annual Convent of the United Grand Lodge of Germany, A.F. & A.M. in 1948, the pin was adopted as an official Masonic emblem honoring those valiant Brethren who carried their work on under adverse conditions. At the Grand Masters Conference in the United States, Dr. Theodor Vogel, the Grand Master of the newly-formed *UGL*, A.F. & A.M., presented one of the pins to each of the representatives of the Grand Jurisdictions with which the *UGL*, A.F. & A.M. enjoyed Fraternal relations.

Thus did a simple flower blossom forth into a meaningful emblem of the Fraternity and become perhaps the most widely worn pin among Freemasons in Germany. In most of our lodges, the Forget-Me-Not is presented to new Master Masons, at which time its history is briefly touched upon.

(*The American-Canadian Trestleboard*)

EXPENSE ACCOUNT

In the Archives of Vincennes Lodge No. 1, Indiana is a "Bill of expenses in going to Corydon, attending the Convention & returning home," which was submitted by General Washington Johnston in December 1817. It includes such necessities as the cost of shoeing his horse, a supply of whisky, the fee for crossing White River on a ferry, and "rum and sugar for journey."

(*The Indiana Freemason*—December 1967)

THE LODGE WHERE I BELONG

Though my Lodge may lack the splendor
Of a temple or a shrine,
Or possess the gaudy fixtures
That are classed as superfine—
Yet the fellowship it offers
Is in price beyond compare
and I wouldn't trade it ever
For life's treasures—rich or rare!

The hand-clasp firm, the word of cheer,
Oh, such meanings they impart:
The mystic ties of brotherhood
That links us, heart to heart!
You'd really have to travel far,
For the friendships quite so strong
As those one always find right here
In the lodge where I belong.

When all my earthly travels end,
And at last I'm borne to rest
Where mortal hands no longer toil
And I cease life's endless quest
Why there's nothing I'd like better—
Should I join the heavenly throng—
Than to meet with all the brothers
Of the Lodge where I belong!

(ARTHUR R. HERRMAN)

VI

"Good humor is the health of the soul, sadness is its poison."

(STANISLAUS)

In one small lodge room they always move the piano to make room for some of the degree work. Everyone pitches in to help—but they're all trying to reach for the stool.

WHAT'S IN A NAME . . .

When M.W. Bro. Elvis A. Mooney, Grand Master of Masons of Missouri, was received with honors and addressed the 49th Assembly of the International Supreme Council of DeMolay, March 16 (1969) at Kansas City, he described to the members and guests the difficulty he had encountered through much of his life because of his first name.

Elvis, often interpreted as a girl's name, caused mix-ups in grade school, high school, and college, where he was sometimes listed as "Miss Elvis."

In World War II Navy he felt the problem solved until the creation of the WAVES. Then again, he began to receive letters and directives addressed to "Miss Elvis Mooney."

After the war, the gyrations of another Elvis, whose last name was Presley, became a sensation on television. Soon the name, Elvis, was a byword from coast to coast.

"Never again was I addressed as a girl," M.W. Master Mooney told his appreciative audience. "I don't know what rock n' roll has done for you," he said, "but it's made a man out of me!"

OUT OF THE MOUTHS OF BABES

The daughter of an ardent Mason had heard her father talk of the "wisdom of Solomon" and of "King Solomon's temple."

"You know why Solomon was so smart?" she said, "Because he had so many wives to advise him."

THE INDISPENSABLE MAN

A Past Master's apron, presented with the usual eulogy, caused one recipient to quote this humbling bit of verse.

Sometime when you're feeling important,
Sometime when your ego's in bloom,
Sometime when you take it for granted
You're the best qualified in the room;
Sometime when you feel that your going
Would leave an unfillable hole
Just follow these simple instructions
And see how they humble your soul.
Take a bucket and fill it with water
Put your hand in it up to the wrist,
Pull it out, and the hole that's remaining
Is a measure of how you'll be missed.
You can splash all you want when you enter,
You may stir up the water galore:
But stop, and you find that in no time
It looks quite the same as before.
The moral in this quaint example
Is to do just the best that you can;
Be proud of yourself, but remember
There's no indispensable man.

HEREAFTER

"You can often tell where one is going hereafter by what he goes after here."

(From *Square and Compass*)

WILL WILLIAMS WILL

In the 1964 Correspondence Report in the *Maine Proceedings,* a typographical error in the review of the Grand Lodge of Georgia caused this sage observation: "Bro. Williams gives us sixty-three will-written reviews."

SKIN HEADS

J. Whitcomb Brougher, D.D., of Glendale, California, a master-orator who served as General Grand Chaplain of the General Grand Council of Royal and Select Masters, peppered his addresses with stories (many of which have been "lifted" for inclusion in this volume). The following quotation from one of his fine addresses should prove useful to many brethren who suffer from receding hairlines:

"Our founding fathers believed in God. We need to renew and revive our faith in God. 'All men are created equal.' You say, 'but we aren't created equal.' Some are tall and some are short. Some are fat and some are thin. Some have hair and . . . nice knowing you! We kid about hair, but a super optimist is the man who is baldheaded and thinks conditions are temporary.

"I grew up in the northwest, and found that the thicker the moss, the rottener the stump! God in his wisdom to all men was fair—to some he gave brains, and to others, hair!"

"From now on I'm going to call you 'Demolay.' . . .'Cause you've sure got a ways to go before you're a Mason!"

THE KEY . . .

A little Masonry may dwell in a great temple, and a great Mason may live in a little upper room over a shop or a store. In the things that matter most, size does not signify and numbers do not count; the spirit is the one thing needful. Without it all else is an elaborate insignificance, an impossible vacuity. What makes Masonry great is its profound faith, its moral idealism, its sincere fellowship, its fruitful and practical service to the common good.

(Author unknown)

LEADERSHIP PROBLEM

There is a story making the rounds about a certain Grand Master who rules his jurisdiction with an iron hand, permitting no deviation from traditional Masonic practices. His word is law to the thousands of Masons in his state, but with all of his leadership ability, he has been unable to persuade his teenage son to get a haircut.

WHAT HAPPENED TO THE DEPUTY?

At the opening of Grand Lodge in England, December 7, 1955, the Earl of Scarbrough, Grand Master, said:

Brethren, I have to offer you the apologies of the Deputy Grand Master, Lord Derby, for his absence. He is required today to attend a police court—as a witness—of course.

BACHELOR EYES

R.E. Grand Prelate Curtis W. V. Junker was a special guest at the Annual Conclave of the Grand Commandery of South Carolina. When it was announced that Dr. Junker was a bachelor, a well known North Carolina lady in attendance said, "That's obvious. His eyes are so peaceful."

(*Knight Templar*—May 1969)

OLD MINUTES

The oldest known Lodge Minutes which record the initiation of a candidate in England are the minutes of a Scottish Lodge some of whose members were in the Scottish Army, invading England, and while there, on May 20, 1641, initiated Robert Moray, or Muray, an officer in the Scottish Army.

(*California Freemason*—Summer 1960)

DIPLOMATIC RECOMMENDATIONS

Gregor MacPherson, Past Grand Master of the District of Columbia, gives us this one:

There are many diplomatic ways of saying unpleasant things that appear to be inoffensive. One never tells another he is a low spirited fellow. He simply says: "I have a minimum high regard for the distinguished gentleman." Or, if he is not particularly impressed by a person or something, he says, "I am underwhelmed."

I maintain a sort of private clipping bureau of my own. These are a few of the items that I have collected from letters of recommendation that have been given to departing employees:

"John Doe worked here for three weeks, and when he left we were satisfied."

"When I hired Smith as manager, he promised I would soon have a going concern. He kept his promise. I am selling the place tomorrow."

"When Miss Jones joined our office staff, I was so overworked that I was going crazy, and she helped me."

(*California Freemason*—Summer 1960)

EXCUSES! EXCUSES!

The High Priest of a Royal Arch Chapter who had been called for jury service asked to be excused.

"On what grounds?" asked the judge.

"My Royal Arch Chapter is host for statewide York Rite Festival, and as High Priest I should be there."

"So, you are one of those men who think you are indispensable; you think your organization can't function without you. Is that it?"

"No sir; far from that. I know very well they can, but I don't want them to find out."

"Excused," said the judge.

"GUILTY BY ASSOCIATION"

When Walter Ulbricht, Communist "boss" in East Germany, ordered a new flag adopted for his Soviet "republic," he unwittingly provided more material for Freemasonry's opponents in Europe who continue the "big lie" attack by associating Freemasonry with Communism.

The new flag substituted a circle for the sickle of the Soviet flag, while retaining the hammer, a Masonic symbol as well as an artisans' tool. Since the circle is also a well-known Masonic symbol, representing in Europe the Supreme Intelligence, it suggested the following idea to a partisan Catholic writer in the *Rheinischer Merkur:*

"The variant Hammer and Sickle leads to the suspicion that Ulbricht is trying to achieve a higher status by using the Masonic symbol of intelligence, the circle. He probably wants to prove that he is the most dependable of all the red satraps, as well as the chief architect of his red Builders State."

While this may seem amusing to some American Freemasons, it is a more serious matter to their German brothers, who face more intolerance and bigotry than we do.

The truth is that Freemasons are still persecuted in Communist East Germany as they are in Roman Catholic Spain.

Die Bruderschaft, official magazine of the United Grand Lodges of Germany, reports that several brothers living in East Germany were arrested after they attended a meeting of the United Grand Lodges in West Berlin. It costs more than dues and assessments to be a Mason in some quarters of the world!

(*California Freemason*—Summer 1960)

BERNARR MACFADDEN'S FUNERAL

Bernarr Macfadden (1868-1955) rose from a humble two-room Missouri farmhouse to a position of wealth, becoming one of the nation's leading publishers. He became better known to millions as a physical culturist. To some he was an eccentric; to others he was a genius born ahead of his time. His extremely active life, which held never a dull moment, verged at times on the bizarre and the sensational, and his funeral continued the pattern. He was given the last rites of the Catholic Church in the hospital, although he was not a Catholic. A Presbyterian minister and a Jewish rabbi conducted the funeral, with members of the Masonic order attending (he had been a member of Publicity Lodge No. 1000, New York City, since 1924).

(*The Royal Arch Mason*—Spring 1969)

WHAT IS FREEMASONRY?

In the home it's kindness
In society, it's courtesy
In business, it's honesty
In work, it's fairness
Toward the unfortunate, it's pity
Toward the wicked, it's resistance
Toward the weak, it's help
Toward the strong, it's trust
Toward the penitent, it's forgiveness
Toward the fortunate, it's congratulations
Toward God, it is reverence and love—
THIS IS MASONRY.

(By Bro. John Cornish, Lodge No. 855, New York—
From the *Empire State Mason,* January-February 1967)

IT TAKES GUTS

When Judge Carl Wahlstrom was Master of his lodge in Worcester, Massachusetts, a young candidate who had had his raising delayed because of intestinal surgery, upon hearing the penalties in the obligation interrupted by asking, "Your honor, I hope this is symbolic?"

CHARITY BEGINS AT HOME

The Grand Master of Arkansas reported addressing a district meeting in Oklahoma on the subject of "Charity, Biblical and Political." He discovered that he was somewhat presumptous when he found that McCurtain County, Oklahoma, had the highest per capita dole of any county in the United States.

(*The Masonic World*—1952)

THE MASONIC WAY

Georgia dedicated a marker to *Samuel Elbert,* who made a valiant stand, March 3, 1779, at the Battle of Brier Creek. In command of 60 Continentals and 160 Militia, surrounded on three sides by the British, he directed one of the most valiant stands in military history. He was about to be killed by the Redcoats when his life was saved by a British officer who was a Mason and who recognized Gen. Elbert as the Grand Master of the Grand Lodge of Georgia. He was later exchanged for a British officer and was with Washington at Yorktown at the surrender of Cornwallis.

THE UNIVERSALITY OF MASONRY

Past Eminent Commander Ryoji Beutner, who is of Japanese and German ancestry, in conferring the Orders of Templary to a class of candidates in Heidelberg Commandery No. 2 (Germany) gave the obligations flawlessly in English, German, Italian and French. Needless to say, he is an expert linguist—speaking some 13 different languages.

"Before I start the interviews, are there any Masons out there?"

SURVIVAL

While he was Meister von Stuhl (Worshipful Master) of Carl zur Eintracht Lodge in Mannhiem, Germany, Wor. Brother Beutner accompanied some of his American brethren to the Annual Convent of the United Grand Lodges of Germany in Berlin. He acted as guide and enthralled them with stories of his life in Berlin during the Hitler regime.

When asked by one of the brethren what he did for a livelihood during the war, Brother Beutner nonchalantly stated, "Oh, I was a salesman—in the black market."

WARRANTY

A monthly newsletter of Frankfurt-on-the-Main Lodge No. 861 (Germany) carried an elaborate certificate:

> WARRANTY
>
> This certificate, together with your paid-up dues card . . . will entitle you to an evening of fellowship at the lodge temple, *any* Monday evening, at 1930 hrs.

FOOD FOR THOUGHT

It is not what we eat, but what we digest . . .
that makes us strong.
It is not what we earn, but what we save . . .
that makes us rich.
It is not what we read, but what we remember . . .
that makes us learned.
It is not what we profess, but what we practice . . .
that makes us Masons!

(BRO. PETE RASMUSSEN, PPGM)

IT'S SO MUCH EASIER . . .

Not to go to Lodge.
Not to concern yourself with others.
Not to participate.
Not to volunteer your aid.
Not to let Masonry pervade your life.
Not to avoid criticizing others.
Not to influence others around you by your
Masonic acts.

WHY BOTHER TO CHANGE?

Your life can only be richer if you do.
Is it worth the effort? . . .
Ask a practicing Brother . . .

(R.W. JESS MINTON)

WANTED

Twenty-two good workmen from Gebal. Short hours of labor, extra good pay in Fellowship. Will you be on hand when called for? Your officers cannot function properly without the strength and support of all Companions. Put on your apron. Pick up your trowel—there is work to be done.

(Harris Council—Massachusetts *R & SM Trestleboard*)

COMMANDER'S MESSAGE

Dear Sir Knights:

When I pass on I hope to leave my son a legacy, but not the kind we generally think of when pondering on such matters.

When my son walks down the street I want people to say, "He has a ready smile, just like his father."

When my son walks into the bank I want people to say, "There is an honest man, just like his father."

When my son relieves the widow and orphan I want people to say, "What a noble and kind man, just like his father."

When my son makes wise decisions in arbitrating the conflicts between his brothers I want people to say, "Such a wise and just man, just like his father."

When my son walks down the street I want people to say, "There goes a Knight Templar, just like his father."

Fraternally yours,
HERBERT W. MATTHEWS,
Eminent Commander.
(Helena Commandery No. 3 KT, New Jersey)

VII

"Some students of Masonry drink at the fountain of knowledge—others just gargle!"

FAMILIAR RING

I met a man the other day,
  A fellow-traveler on life's way;
Our paths had never crossed before,
  And maybe we shall meet no more
At least not this side heaven's gates
  Where the great Architect awaits—
He bore no mark of wealth or fame,
  Perhaps he'd won no great acclaim,
Upon his hand he wore a ring—
  'Twas not a costly jewelled thing—
But there an emblem plainly shown
  Told me that I was not alone,
For as we stood together there
  I knew that he was on the square.

(BRO. BRIGADIER GEORGE CREWE)

SIR KNIGHT

In 1886, the famed American poetess Ella Wheeler Wilcox, wrote the following poem for a Public Installation of St. Elmo Commandery No. 9, Knights Templar, Meridian, Connecticut. We offer it because every Freemason should live up to the sentiments expressed therein.

I

Sir Knight of the world's oldest order,
  Sir Knight of the Army of God,
You have crossed the strange mystical border,
  The ground flood of truth you have trod;
    You have entered the Sanctum Sanctorum,

Which leads to the temple above,
        Where you come as a stone,
        And a Christ-chosen one,
In the kingdom of Friendship and Love.

II

As you stand in this new realm of beauty,
    Where each man you meet is your friend,
Think not that your promise of duty
    In hall, or asylum, shall end;
        Outside in the great world of pleasure,
Beyond, in the clamor of trade,
        In the battle of life,
        And its course daily strife,
Remember the vows you have made.

III

Your service, majestic and solemn,
    Your symbols, suggestive and sweet,
Your uniformed phalanx in column
    On gala days marching the street;
        Your sword and your plume and your helmet
Your "secrets" hid from the world's sight;
        These things are the small,
        Lesser parts of the all
Which are needed to form the true Knight.

IV

The martyrs who perished rejoicing
    In Templary's glorious laws.
Who died 'midst the fagots while voicing
    The glory and worth of their cause—
        They honored the title of "Templar"
No more than the Knight of to-day,
        Who mars not the name
        With one blemish of shame
But carries it clean through life's fray.

V

To live for a cause, to endeavor
    To make your deeds grace it, to try

And uphold its precepts forever,
Is harder by far than to die!
For the battle of life is unending,
The enemy, Self, never tires,
And the true Knight must slay
That sly foe every day,
Ere he reaches the heights he desires.

VI

Sir Knight, have you pondered the meaning
Of all you have heard and been told?
Have you strengthened your heart for its weaning
From vices and faults loved of old?
Will you honor, in hours of temptation,
Your promises, noble and grand?
Will your spirit be strong
To do battle with wrong,
"And having done all, to stand?"

VII

Will you ever be true to a brother
In actions as well as in creed?
Will you stand by his side as no other
Could stand in the hour of his need?
Will you boldly defend him from peril,
And lift from him poverty's curse—
Will the promise of aid
Which you willingly made,
Reach down from your lips to your purse?

VIII

The world's battle field is before you!
Let wisdom walk close by your side,
Let Faith spread her snowy wings o'er you,
Let truth be your comrade and guide;
Let Fortitude, Justice and Mercy
Direct all your conduct aright,
And let each word and act
Tell to men the proud fact
You're worthy the name of "Sir Knight."

"I take it your article was printed in The Royal Arch Mason?"

LETTER TO THE EDITOR

The following is extracted from a letter to the editor of *The Cabletow* (Grand Lodge of the Philippines) from J. Bar-Ner, the Grand Secretary of the Grand Lodge of Israel:

For the sake of the record, our Grand Lodge was erected and consecrated by the Grand Lodge of Scotland in the year 1953 and today numbers 57 lodges which work in the following languages.

Hebrew—The language of our Grand Lodge.

English, Arabic, French, German and Rumanian. We are also proud that in our Jurisdiction, Brethren of all creeds, Jew, Gentile, Arab are to be found in the lodges. Further, in lodges where Brethren (or initiates) are of different Faiths the holy Books of the three great faiths—Old Testament, New Testament and the Koran are to be found on our altars.

ZIP CODES OMITTED

According to Alphonse Cerza, in his article "The Truth Is Stranger Than Fiction," published by the Masonic Service Association, September, 1967, some places and streets bear names that have Masonic significance. Some may be merely a coincidence; others may have been named because of a Masonic connection. For example: *Anchor,* Illinois; *Beehive,* Montana: *Boaz,* Alabama; *Charity,* Missouri; *Circle,* Montana; *Cowan,* Tennessee; *Emblem,* Wyoming; *Eureka,* West Virginia; *Faith,* South Dakota; *False Pass,* Alaska; *Fidelity,* Illinois; *Five Points,* Alabama and Tennessee; *Freeborn,* Minnesota; *Grand Pass,* Missouri; *Grotto,* Washington; *Hiram,*

Maine and Ohio; *Hope,* Alaska and Minnesota; *Jachin,* Alabama; *Justice,* Illinois; *Lodge,* South Carolina; *Mason,* Kentucky; *Mason City,* Iowa; *Masonic Home,* Kentucky; *Masontown,* West Virginia; *Medinah,* Illinois (after Shrine Temple in Chicago); *Mount Moriah,* Missouri; *Red Jacket,* West Virginia; *Square,* Montana; *Sophia,* West Virginia; *Steward,* Illinois; *Symbol,* Kentucky; *Temperance,* Michigan; *Tyler,* Texas; *Wisdom,* Montana.

There is an *Acacia Road* in Milwaukee, Wisconsin. There is a *Mason Street* in Boise, Idaho; Chicago, Illinois; Evanston, Illinois; Joliet, Illinois; Milwaukee, Wisconsin; and Springfield, Illinois. Norfolk, Virginia, has a *Freemasons Street.* There is a *Masonic Avenue* in San Francisco, California.

THE HONEYMOON IS OVER

The following notice in *The Al Malaikahan,* official publication of the Al Malaikah Temple, AAONMS, makes it official.

There will not be any Honeymoon Ceremonial this year or any year. There never has been a Honeymoon Ceremonial held by Al Malaikah Temple, or any other Temple of the Order of the Mystic Shrine. Every Ceremonial is, has been and will be strictly stag.

Many members of the Nobility confuse Honeymoon Pilgrimages with Honeymoon Ceremonials. There are excursions, expeditions or pilgrimages to cities where Ceremonials are held, and on some of these junkets the distaff side is invited by the Potentate.

Mistakenly, some Nobles refer to these pilgrimages which include the Ladies as "HONEYMOON CEREMONIALS." The Pilgrimage is conducted for the purpose of the Ceremonial; and if the fair daughters of the desert are invited to join the caravan and it becomes a "Honeymoon Pilgrimage" their presence is incidental to the Ceremonial, the ceremony of induction of new members into the ranks of the Nobility.

Nobles should never refer to a Ceremonial as a "Stag Ceremonial." All Ceremonials are STAG. Pilgrimages may be STAG or HONEYMOON at the will and pleasure of the Potentate. But no Potentate, not even the Imperial Potentate can declare a "Honeymoon Ceremonial."

TAKE TIME

Take Time TO THINK . . .
It is the source of power.

Take Time TO PLAY . . .
  It is the secret of perpetual youth.
Take Time TO READ . . .
  It is the fountain of wisdom.
Take Time TO PRAY . . .
  It is the greatest power on earth.
Take Time TO LOVE AND BE LOVED . . .
  It is a God-given privilege.
Take Time TO BE FRIENDLY . . .
  It is the road to happiness.
Take Time TO LAUGH . . .
  It is the music of the soul.
Take Time TO GIVE . . .
  It is too short a day to be selfish.
Take Time TO WORK . . .
  It is the price of success.
Take Time TO BE A MASON . . .

  Follow a compass charted course to new adventures
  in the York and Scottish Rites and
Revel in the fun of helping a child
TO walk as a Shriner . . .
  It is the wholesomeness of life.

(Author Unknown)

TO A PAST MASTER

Who's the stranger, Mother dear?
Look, he knows us—ain't he queer?
Hush, my son, don't talk so wild;
He's your father, dearest child.
He's my father? It's not so.
Father died eight years ago.
Dad didn't die, O child of mine;
He's been going through "The Line."
But, he's been Master now, so he
Has no place to go, you see—
No place left for him to roam—
That's why he's coming home.

(Bro. Walter K. Belt—
The Oregon Freemason)

CARPET SAVER

A sign in the anteroom of a lodge in a Maine logging town reads: HOBNAIL BOOTS NOT ALLOWED IN LODGEROOM.

PROFICIENT COMMITTEE

The visitor arrived at a small Virginia lodge early and requested to be examined. Two Past Masters and a newly raised Mason served on the Committee. The visitor was really put through the paces as the Past Masters used the examination as an instruction tool for the other member.

After the extensive examination, the visitor signed the register, listing his title as a grand officer in a sister jurisdiction.

After the lodge was opened, it fell the lot of one of the Past Masters who had served on the Committee to present the distinguished visitor. In presenting and introducing him, he said, "I am pleased to inform you that our Right Worshipful Brother has examined your Examining Committee and found them proficient."

MADISON AVENUE

The Scottish Rite Bodies in Connecticut lean heavily on modern advertising techniques:

"To get the greatest enjoyment out of worthwhile things requires some personal involvement—a little of your time and effort. Isn't it a thrill to see the friend and brother you have signed-up sitting with the candidates? Ours is not just a dues-paying fraternity. We thrive on people, all volunteers, who are interested in seeing and talking about a better way-of-life. It is possible if YOU join with us in our crusade. We try to supply the finest facilities. We have comfortable seats, ample room and all in living color. Ours is a program of real live people—your friends and brothers!

A STINKING MEETING

Pioneer Lodge, located at Somerset, Massachusetts, recently observed its centennial. One of the old records had the following notation:

"At this point the Worshipful Master interrupted the meeting to ascertain the source and character of certain obnoxious gases irritating the olfactories and apparently emanating from the culinary regions below. Upon investigation by the Inside Sentinel it was found that certain hydrocarbons were pouring from incompletely closed jets. The correction of the condition was immediate; no damage was done; no one indicted for dereliction of duty, and the deliberations resumed."

CREATURE COMFORT

Past Grand Master Ray Rideout tells of the time that he was the speaker at one of his Maine lodges. The Master had gone pretty much through the program and finally he turned to the Grand Master and said, "Do you want to speak now or will I let the boys be comfortable a while longer?"

TO WIT

From a meeting notice of Warren Lodge of Amesbury, Massachusetts, we lifted this bit of "legal talk":

"It would seem that a return to those fundamental principles which were transmitted to us by our Masonic forefathers, to have and to hold, with all the rights thereto belonging, unto us, our heirs and assigns forever, upon which this and other lodges have grown and made the influence of Masonry felt during the past centuries is what we need most today."

PRESCRIBED UNIFORM

The "Summons" of Benjamin Franklin Lodge No. 52, a military lodge of the Grand Lodge Nationale Francais, invariably had this notation:

DRESS

Officers: Dinner jacket and white gloves.

Members and Visitors: Dinner jacket or dark business suit or Class "A" uniform, white gloves.

CASTING A SPELL

In two successive issues of the *Trestleboard* of Manitou Lodge No. 68 of Colorado, the Master's message was addressed, "Dear Brethers," and "Dear brothern." Other interesting spellings in the same messages were: "philosoply," "encreasing," "intertainment," "refteshments," and "lucheon."

THEY DID! HE DID!

They tell an interesting story about how TAHATTAWAN Lodge in Littleton, Massachusetts, got its new temple—a former Roman

Catholic church. It seems that when a large new Catholic church was built in town, the old one was put up for sale. The lodge needed new quarters, but could not afford the amount asked for the vacant church. In fact it was lacking about $50,000 of the price tag.

One night, though, as the brethren were gathering to open in their old, cramped, rented quarters, one of the members came in with the news that a little girl had been hit by a car and the hospital had an urgent need for whole blood. The lodge was some three hours late in opening because everyone went to the hospital to donate a pint of blood.

When word of this reached Cardinal Cushing, it is reported that he said, in effect, "If the Masons can respond like that for one of ours, we can knock $50,000 off the price of that church—if they still want it."

They did! And he did!

NOT THE END OF THE STORY

To convert the Catholic Church into a Masonic Temple took a lot of work by the members of TAHATTAWAN Lodge who did much of their own remodelling. The "Stations of the Cross" which were painted on the walls were neatly painted over with Squares and Compasses. The pews were removed and the Master's and Warden's stations were constructed. While the work was going on, curious parishioners who had formerly worshipped there, stopped by to see the work progress, including Father Murphy.

One day after a hole for the light over the altar had been made, one curious visitor asked what the hole in the ceiling was for.

"Oh!" answered one of the volunteer workers, "When Father Murphy came in today and saw what we had done to the 'Stations of the Cross,' he went right through the roof."

VIII

"A smile is the whisper of a laugh."

Conrad Hahn, who guides the helm of the Masonic Service Association of the U.S., and is one of Masonry's foremost speakers, had this to say in his annual address when he was Grand Master of Connecticut:

"In an almost exclusively feminine household there are, as some of you can imagine, certain misconceptions about my Masonic activities; but the only serious objection to the situation seems to be directed against our masculine exclusiveness, which forbids the making of a woman a Mason. My dear ladies have pointed out that Scriptures approve of women becoming Masons, because it is recorded in the book of Genesis that after Adam and Eve had eaten of the forbidden fruit and discovered their nakedness, 'they sewed fig leaves together and made themselves aprons.' "

KALEIDOSCOPE OR MAYBE ROSE COLORED GLASSES

Dean C. Settle, Grand Secretary of the Grand Lodge of Colorado, penned these words in the *Colorado Masonic Craftsman* (January 1968).

Wasn't there a time when—

—Most elders demanded respect from their children

—Police officers were considered a stalwart friend of the community

—Majority rule was the order of the day

—Minority did not mean total disrespect for law and order

—No one expected "Flower Power" to solve the major issues of the time

—Some people took a bath every Saturday night whether they needed it or not

—Civil Rights did not destroy human rights

—Welfare denoted a time of emergency, not a way of life

—LSD could have stood for Let's Save Democracy

—Most movies were either comedies or a wholesome family life story.

Really, yours truly is no pessimist, but a little reflection can be good at times. We have a great deal to be thankful for today. Our friends are most valuable assets and the fellowship in the Fraternity offers us the opportunity to increase our friendship circle every day.

We at the Grand Lodge Office invite you to come and see us. Give us the opportunity of helping you along the Masonic path.

LIGHT YOUR LIGHT!

Let's be a Mason every day,
  Not only on Tuesday night;
For it's being a Mason all the while
  That gives our Craft its Light.
  (RONALD HAHN—*Trestleboard*—
  Alt Heidelberg Lodge No. 821—March 1961)

DID YOU KNOW?

One of the only two streets in the United States named Freemason Street is in Norfolk, Virginia. Originally laid out as a road in 1762, it became a street as the city developed and lacking a name, was designated Freemason Street because of the Freemason Lodge building located on it.

* * *

The first Masonic Lodge south of the equator was organized at Cape Town, South Africa, in 1772, then a part of a Dutch colony, and was chartered by the Grand East of the Netherlands. History records that its ceremonies were conducted in either Dutch, French or English, depending on the language of the candidate.

THE CASTLE IN THE DISTANCE

There is an old story which gives us a lesson for today.

A poor little boy once lived in a weatherworn cottage on the top of a hill. Every day at sunset he would sit on the doorstep and look down the road, fascinated by a beautiful house at the far side of the valley. He was greatly dissatisfied with the poverty of his own surroundings, and the sight of the house in the valley, where he had never been, made him very unhappy.

"If I could just live in that beautiful house with the wonderful golden windows, how happy I should be," he said.

The boy made up his mind to go and visit the beautiful house. So early one morning he started out. The road was dusty, and soon the sun was hot, but the little traveller trudged on and on. At length, near the end of the day he found himself at the far side of the valley. But what he stood looking at was only an old tumble-down barn. And the windows were not gold at all, but just ordinary glass, and dirty and broken, too. Tired and thirsty, the boy flung himself on the ground and wept bitterly.

When he arose he saw his own cottage on the hill top, and in the light of the setting sun, the windows were shining as if they were covered with blazing gold.

(By V. M. Burrows—*The New Mexico Freemason*)

DEBTS

Bro. Benjamin Franklin had these things to say about debt.

He that goes a-borrowing goes a-sorrowing.

If you'd be wealthy, think more of saving than of getting.

Beware of small expenses: a leak will sink a great ship.

'Tis against some men's principle to pay interest, and it seems against others' interest to pay the principal.

Rather go to bed supperless than run into debt for a breakfast.

Spare and have is better than spend and crave.

It is hard for any empty sack to stand upright.

BOSOM BEATING

I am getting weary of the endless bosom-beating over the lack of lodge attendance. Whatever is wrong with lodge attendance today was wrong 26 years ago when I became a Mason, and it was wrong the year I was Master of my lodge. There were times when it was difficult to get enough out to open lodge. But looking back on that year, I have to admit that much of the trouble was my own fault. Some of my meetings were such a bore that I go to almost any length to avoid attending that kind of meeting today. When I actually made an effort to prepare a lodge activity that was worthwhile—*and truly Masonic in character*—I had no trouble filling the chairs.

(M.W. Bro. Dwight L. Smith, *Indiana Proceedings*—1960)

UP YONDER

Texas appears to be the only jurisdiction which has an official Grand Lodge song; it is used at the opening and closing of most of their communications; its title—"When the Roll Is Called Up Yonder."

DAFFYNITION

A wag defined a Masonic banquet as an affair where a speaker eats a lot of food he doesn't want, then talks about something he doesn't know much about, to a lot of brothers who don't want to hear him.

"Now be sure to comment on his elevation to a thirty-third degree Mason."

THE GREAT LIGHT

Lieutenant Governor Arthur W. Coolidge, Past Grand Master of Massachusetts, told of an occasion where he attended a convention and the manager of the hotel had given him a room in which to change his clothes; this he did in a very few minutes. During that time he saw on the table beside him a Gideon Bible. On the fly leaf he noticed a very interesting inscription:

"If you are away from home, read Moses. If you are despondent, read the Psalms. If you are lonesome read about Joseph."

Underneath these words another individual had written:

"If you are still lonesome call 624-1168, and ask for *Mary.*

SICKNESS AND DISTRESS

This from the *Virginia Masonic Herald:*

Editor's Note.—The report from Ruth Lodge is rather brief this month due to Brother Mason being confined to the hospital. His address is: General Hospital, Maternity Section, Norfolk, Virginia. The good brother has a swelling—in his foot.

Looks as if the good brother is out of his element!

I BELIEVE

Our gratitude for the little things of today is felt by every Brother, and here is a list of the Best Words to live by: *Courteous* words instead of sharp remarks; *smiles* instead of blank looks; *enthusiasm* instead of a closed mind; *attention* instead of neglect; *patience* instead of irritation; *sincerity* instead of shame; *consideration* instead of annoyance. *Remembering people* instead of forgetting; *facts* instead of arguments; *helpfulness* instead of hindrance; *action* instead of delay; *appreciation* instead of apathy.

(ALEXANDER V. HOULON 32°, Alexandria, Va.)

IT'S LATER THAN YOU THINK

Everything is farther than it used to be. It's twice as far to the lodge, for instance, and they've added a hill, I've noticed. I've given up running for my bus, it leaves faster than it used to. Seems to me they are making staircases steeper than they used to make them in the old days. And have you noticed the small print they are using? Newspapers are getting farther away when I hold them and I have to squint to make out the news. No sense in asking to have them read aloud, everyone speaks in such a low voice that I can hardly hear them. The barber doesn't hold a mirror behind me any more so that I can see the back of my head. The strings on the aprons at lodge are shorter than they used to be. The material in my suit is always too skimpy around the waist and the seat. Even my shoe laces are so short they are all but impossible to reach. Even people are changing, they are so much younger than they used to be when I was their age. On the other hand, people my own age are so much older than I am. I ran into an old classmate the other night and he had aged so he didn't recognize me. I got to thinking about the poor old fellow while I was shaving this morning, and while doing so I glanced at my own reflection in the mirror. Confound it, they don't even use the same kind of glass in the mirrors any more!

NEED OF CONTACT

One candle may light another provided there is contact. One candle will never light another at a distance—only when flame touches wick. One Brother may kindle the fire of another, but not by standing aloof and away—only by intimate contact of mind with mind and heart with heart may the fire pass from man to man. Is the gentle but powerful Light of Masonry Shining from you?

SHAKING EXPERIENCE

The Grand Historian in Washington reported:

"We are told that the most severe earthquake ever experienced in Olympia occurred one night while a candidate was kneeling at the altar, blindfolded. The candidate was one Ben Turner, a typical logger of the early days who, as they say, used to swear by note. When the quake hit the building everyone ran out, leaving Ben alone, still kneeling. After it was over they returned and found him in the same position, and asked him if he had not been afraid. He said, 'No, I felt a trembling sensation, but as I came prepared to get hell, I figured I was getting it.' For all his profanity, Ben was a real Mason and a credit to his lodge."

DO YOU "JUST BELONG"

Are you an active member
the kind that would be missed
or are you just contented
that your name is on the list?

Do you attend the meetings
and mingle with the flock
or do you stay at home
and criticize and knock?

Do you take an active part
to help the work along
are you satisfied to be
the kind that "JUST BELONG"?

Do you ever go and visit
a member that is sick
or leave the work to a few
and talk about the clique?

Think this over, member,
you know right from wrong
are you an active member
or do you "JUST BELONG"?

ARX YOU A KXY PXRSON?

Xvxn though my typxwritxr is an old modxl it works quitx wxll xxcxpt for onx of thx kxys. I havx wishxd many timxs that it workxd pxrfxctly; it is trux that thxrx arx 46 kxys that function wxll xnough but just onx kxy not working makxs thx diffxrxncx. Sometimxs it sxxms to mx that cxrtain of our mxmbxrs arx somxwhat likx my typxwritxr; not all thx kxy pxoplx arx working propxrly. You may say to yoursxlf: "Wxll, I am only onx pxrson; It won't makx or brxak thx Ritx." But it doxs makx a diffxrxncx bxcausx thx ritx to bx xffxctivx, nxxds thx activx participation of xvxry mxmbxr. So thx nxxt timx you think you arx only onx pxrson and that your xfforts arxn't nxxdxd, rxmxmbxr my typxwritxr and say to yoursxlf: "I am a kxy pxrson in thx Ritx and I am nxxdxd."

(*Rochester SR News*)

IF WITHIN THE LENGTH OF HIS CABLETOW

In 1741, the *Earl of Rosse* fell sick and was not expected to live. While he had served as Grand Master of Freemasons in Ireland, his doings were not entirely above reproach, and so conspicuous a sinner was a fair mark for the well meant admonitions of the clergy, whom he had often shocked by some of his excesses; the gossip of the day was full of stories of the Earl's witty perversity under exhortations . . . twice, it would seem, during this fatal illness, benevolent clergymen made zealous efforts to recall the "transgressor" to the paths of righteousness. On the first occasion, the pious minister (they are always so-called), who had made his way to the bedside of the dying Earl, concluded an eloquent appeal, adjuring him to call on the Lord.

The Earl found strength enough to reply, with awful flippancy:

I doubt, reverend sir, if I be going that way; but if I do chance to find myself in his neighborhood, I will make sure of calling on his Lordship.

"You don't say! Why I'm a Mason myself!"

THE CALL TO SERVICE

Let me relate an experience of mine.
In a manner so valiant and sublime,
A signal honor was conferred upon me,
Knighthood in the Order of Templary.

Now I'm arrayed in Templar black,
With stripped belt around the back,
Chapeau and crest, with plume of white,
Armed with the sword so shining bright.

Wearing the Chapeau with honor and pride,
Its symbol of purity never denied;
Uncovering in moments of devotion and prayer,
Kneeling before God with head bowed there.

Carrying the sword with a steady hand,
Obeying the order of one in command;
Always remembering that every true Knight
Draws it only in defense of the right.

Thus is Templary around the world,
Marching for Christ with banner unfurled,
Noted for deeds of kindness and love,
Following the example of our Commander above.

And so should all knights with ready ear
Hear the command of our Savior clear;
"Be true! Be vigilant!, no matter the loss,
There is no crown, without the cross!"

(The above was written by The Reverend Ernest G. Rice, Superintendent of the West Virginia Masonic Home. He is Eminent Commander of Calvary Commandery No. 3, Parkersburg, West Virginia.)

(*Knight Templar,* July 1969)

JUDGE KINDLY

Don't expect perfection in a man just because he is a Mason. If you do, you will be disappointed. Masonry makes men better, but no human agency makes them perfect. If he is a Mason, you have a right to presume he is a fairly good man, but do not condemn Masonry even if a few Masons turn out bad. Even the Great Teacher himself had a Judas. The aim and purpose of Masonry is to receive none but good men, keep them good, and make them better. Judge the Institution, not by a few failures, but by the average of its successes. That average is high and it consequently gives standing to its members, but it cannot be an infallible guide.

The Fraternity may decide to do something which you, as an individual member, may oppose. But do not feel that you must condemn the action on that account. You may be right but do not pull away. Even you are not infallible, and the Institution has stood for so many years, you may feel assured that its average performance will be good.

(*Indiana Freemason*)

PAPA AND MAMMA

"Gracious, Fanny!" exclaimed a mother to her small daughter, "why are you shouting like that? Why can't you be quiet like your brother?"

"He's got to be quiet," replied Fanny. "He's playing papa coming home late from the lodge."

"And who are you playing, pray tell?"

"Oh, I'm playing I'm you."

THE AWAKENING

"John!" she exclaimed, jabbing her elbow into his ribs at two o'clock in the morning, "did you lock the kitchen door?"

"Worthy Ruler, our portals are guarded," said John, as he made the proper sign and went back to sleep.

SAVE A GOOD ONE

At an entertainment in Chicago, the speaker of the evening stressed the main topic of his address and said "one purpose of our noble Fraternity is to save young men."

A sweet young lady in the audience leaned over and shispered to the older brother sitting in front of her: "Tell 'em to save a good one for me, please."

IX

"What sunshine is to flowers, smiles are to humanity."

HIGH BRASS

The late Frank M. Totton, Past Grand Master of New York, introducing Chaplain Charles D. Broughton of Buffalo, told this story:

"They told me when he graduated from Seminary his first church was a very small one up in a small town in New York. He didn't have the silk stocking church he has now, just a small church, but he became very popular in that town almost overnight, so popular in fact that they invited him to join a noon-day luncheon club three weeks after he came to town. Shortly after that they had the annual election, and they waited upon him and asked him if he would accept election as an officer. He said, 'What do you want me to be?'

"They said, 'We want you to be hog caller.'

"Dr. Broughton said, 'Hog caller? No, I couldn't do that.'

"They said, 'Well, it is a very important office in this club. We have a president, vice-president, treasurer and hog caller, so you can see it is quite high brass.'

"Finally, they prevailed on Brother Broughton to accept and he said, 'Well, all right, if you want me to be hog caller, why, hog caller it is, but I must confess to you folks that when I came to town a few months ago I had hoped that some day I might be known as the shepherd of the sheep, but certainly you folks know your own people better than I do.' "

TEMPERANCE IS A VIRTUE

"It will be interesting at this point to consider what this and other lodges were like 200 years ago. The members had the use of one room in the tavern, where they carried out their ceremonies and subsequently had a meal. At first they wore plain leather aprons, but later in the century some ornamentation was added. These plain aprons were given to the initiates and were bought at a cost of 1/ to 1/6 pence each. Wine and punch were drunk in the lodge, and any consumed while the lodge was open was paid for from lodge funds. Here is an extract from the minutes of October 28, 1767:

" 'The Irregularities and other ill consequences of Ebriety which strike at the Root of our well grounded Order having been often beheld by the Brethren of this Lodge of Masons, (Antiquity Lodge) particularly at our last Meeting with proper detestation. To prevent such ill effects for the future, it is this Night unanimously determined that no Brother be permitted to drink more in the Lodge or during Lodge Hours than one Pint of Wine or one Shillings worth of Punch or Brandy or Rum and Water. Such Wine to be of the Common sort at 2 Shillings per Bottle unless any Bro. choosing Wine of a higher price or having his Pint made into Negus shall make up the Difference from his own Purse over and above the usual Contributions to the Lodge, but on no Account be permitted to drink more, so long as the Lodge shall be open, or afterwards at the Lodges Expense—nor shall more than two join in their Liquor and not those unless they sit together upon the Penalty of 2/6 for every Breach of any Part of this Order, Malt Liquor with Suppers, only excepted.' "

(Extract from *The Collected Prestonian Lectures,* 1925-1960, published by Quatuor Coronati Lodge No. 2076, England.)

SPELLIN' BEE

An examination of Grand Lodge proceedings shows that grand secretaries (or is it the printer) have not improved in their spelling.

Several jurisdictions have "grand *marshalls.*"

One jurisdiction has a grand "*herold.*"

Another jurisdiction introduces an "Emminent" frater.

Another proceedings has a "cronology."

A grand master, speaking before a grand lodge refers in two or three places in his address to the "die-us." He probably meant "day-us," which is the platform in the east. (Spelled *Dais.*)

And the words *"Grand* jurisdictions" are being thrown around by speakers and writers until we have almost come to the belief that there are some very grand jurisdictions.

Too many high-falutin titles do these Freemasons have. What we need is a Masonic "eliminator" for titles.

WHAT'S IN A NAME?

The South Weymouth (Massachusetts) Naval Air Station is the home of the well-known "Ebb and Flow Degree Team."

* * *

"Semper Paratus," the U.S. Coast Guard motto, is the name of a lodge in Washington, D.C., which is made up primarily of members of the Coast Guard.

* * *

Wild Cat Lodge No. 311, in Indiana—must have really been wild. It lost its charter.

"Looks like Harry's out for volunteers again."

LET GEORGE DO IT!

Some members keep their Chapter strong,
While others join and just belong;
Some dig right in, some serve with pride,
Some go along, just for the ride.
Some volunteer to do their share,
While some lay back and just don't care;
On meeting nights some always show
While there are those who never go.
Some always pay their dues ahead,
Some get behind for months, instead.
Some do their best, some build, some make,
Some never give, but always take,
Some drag, some pull, some don't, some do.
CONSIDER, which of these are you?

POWER OF THE PRESS

An Oregon newspaper describing the grand lodge session in Portland announced that—

Walter Winslow was re-elected to a five-year term on the *juris-produce* committee.

The new Grand Master is said to be a member of the Scottish and *Yoke* Rite.

THE COMMON POOL

Deep in the poppies on Flanders field,
  At the close of a gory day,
With prayers said—and courage steeled
  Three dying soldiers lay.

On the breast of one was the York Rite Crest
  On another, just the Compass and Square,
While the stiffening hand of the other pressed
  The Scottish double eagle en flare.

All-for-one and one-for-all
  Each had fought for his country's good.
They smiled as their Blood formed A Common Pool,
They smiled—for each understood.

(THOMAS WILLING HICKS)

WHAT IS A MASON?

A MASON is a MAN and BROTHER whose TRUST is in God. He meets you on the LEVEL and acts upon the SQUARE. Truth is his COMPASS and he is ever PLUMB. He has a true GRIP on all that is RITE. He is loyal to his ORDER and whatever his DEGREE, he is MASTER of himself. In the LODGE of Life he wears unstained the white LAMB SKIN of Innocence. From his INITIATION as an ENTERED APPRENTICE he travels ever East toward the LIGHT of WISDOM until he receives the final—the DIVINE INEFFABLE PRESENCE OF THE ETERNAL SUPREME GRAND MASTER OF THE UNIVERSE.

GOD

(OSCAR A. DELONG)

A MASON AND A MAN

Brother, Masonry means much more
  Than the wearing of a pin,
Or carrying a paid up dues receipt
    So that the Lodge will let you in.

You can wear an emblem in your coat,
  From your finger flash a ring,
But if you are not sincere at heart
  This doesn't mean a thing.

It is merely an outward sign
  To show the world that you belong,
To that great fraternal brotherhood
  That teaches right from wrong.

What really counts lies buried deep
  Within the human breast,
Till Masonic teaching brings it out
  And puts it to the test.

If you practice out of Lodge
  The things you learn within,
Be just and upright to yourself
  And to your fellowmen.

Console a brother when he's sick,
  Assist him when in need,
Without a thought of personal reward
  For any act or deed.

Walk and act in such a way
  The world without will see,
That only the best can meet the test
  Laid down by Masonry.

Be always faithful to your trust
  And do the best you can,
Then you can proudly tell the world
  You're a Mason and a man.

THE LAMBSKIN

It is not ornamental, its cost is not great
There are things far more useful, yet truly I state
That of all my possessions, none can compare
With The White Leathern Apron, that all Masons wear
As a young lad I wondered, just what it all meant
When Dad hustled around and so much time was spent
In shaving and dressing, and looking just right
Until Mother would say, "It's the Masons tonight."

Sometimes Mother would say, "What makes you go,
Way up there tonight, through the sleet and snow;
You see the same things each month of the year."
And then Dad would say, "Yes, I know my Dear,
Each time I see the same things, it is true,
Though they be old, they always seem new;
For each hand that I clasp, each friend that I greet
Seem just a little closer, each time we meet."
Years later I stood at that very same door,
With good men and true, who had entered before,
Kneeled at the Altar and there I was taught,
That Virtue and Honor can never be bought.
That there on the level, men meet and abide,
That wealth and position is all cast aside.
So Honor the Lambskin and may it remain,
Forever unblemished and free from all stain.
So that when we are called to the Grand Architect's Love
We will meet Him up there, in that Grand Lodge above.

DISCOVERED BY RUSSIA

Soviet writer Boris Gorbatov, in an article appearing in the October 2, 1947 issue of the *St. Louis Post-Dispatch* had this to say about M.W. Bro. Harry S Truman, who was then President of the United States: "It is known on trustworthy authority that he was a Mason."

He went on to describe our famous brother: "A man who loves bow ties, wears his pants two inches shorter than ordinary, and who has other external marks of distinction. . . . He has a colorless Baptist face that causes so much trouble to retouchers of *Life,* and it was known that he is most average of all Americans and most provincial of all Missourians."

Rather hard on Missourians—not to mention the "colorless Baptists."

ON THE HIGH WIRE

An officer of the Grand Lodge of South Carolina told the following story a few years ago to the Grand Lodge of Virginia:

"A brother attended Grand Lodge for the first time a number of years ago. He said, 'Who are those distinguished gentlemen in the East?' I said, 'My brother, they are Past Grand Masters. They have served their terms and are even now in the Grand Lodge to lend their help and support to the Grand Master." He replied, 'Well, they remind me of something we have on the farm.' I asked, 'What is that?' He said, 'When we go to the lower pasture, we have a high wire fence on the back of the pasture, and on top of that top wire is a row of vultures, commonly called buzzards; these buzzards swoop down and tear anything to pieces that is offered.' "

ARE YOUR DUES PAID?

After the lodges in Germany were dissolved by the Nazis, they found in the records of the various lodges the names and addresses of the brethren who were in arrears. The authorities ordered the Polizei (police) to collect the back dues, which were then turned into the public treasury, to join the lodge funds already confiscated.

CONDENSED VERSION

Foreign Correspondents of many grand lodges completely review the proceedings of all of the other jurisdictions. In the report of one Fraternal Correspondent, the Foreword contained these comments:

"Old soldiers never die, they just fade away," but old reviewers never die, they merely peter-out. A complete review was an impossibility this year due to various causes physical and otherwise. Instead, a review of nine jurisdictions is herewith presented and the selection was made on the following basis:

A Small, but scattered Jurisdiction—York Grand Lodge of Mexico.
An Unusual Jurisdiction—Pennsylvania.
A British Jurisdiction—Ireland.
A Western Jurisdiction—California
An Old Jurisdiction—South Carolina.
A Young Jurisdiction—Oklahoma.
A Small Jurisdiction—Utah.
A Canadian Jurisdiction— Canada (Ontario).
A Large Jurisdiction—New York.

Oklahoma is not a young jurisdiction in the exact meaning of that word, but as a United Grand Lodge it is.

Ireland was selected instead of Scotland or England because we hear very little about it.

South Carolina was selected instead of Massachusetts because the proceedings were at hand and the Massachusetts proceedings were not.

Mexico was selected because of the unusual situation existing there.

Australia should have been included with one of the Grand Lodges there and so should Europe, but it is too late now to do anything about it.

Other reviewers the world around may express regret at such a limited view of Masonry, but they should be grateful not to have to wade through a complete review such as this reviewer would write.

A SMILING PRAYER

"Give us, O Lord, a bit of sun,
A bit of work and a bit of fun,
Give us all in the struggle and sputter
Our daily bread and a bit of butter.
Give us our health, our keep to make.
And a bit to spare for poor folks' sake.
Give us sense for we're some of us duffers
And a heart to feel for all that suffers.
Give us, too, a bit of song
And a tale, and a book to help us along.
And give us our share of sorrow's lesson,
That we may prove how grief's a blessing.
Give us, O Lord, a chance to be
Our goodly best, brave, wise and free
Our goodly best for ourselves and others
'Til all men learn to live as brothers."

THE EXAMINATION

Brother Dr. Harry Goldwag of New York, on a visit to one of the Tel Aviv lodges, was witness to the strict examination guests were subjected to before being permitted to enter the lodge. In this connection he told us of what had once occurred when he visited a lodge in Philadelphia and was not allowed to enter until he had passed an examination. He was asked about all the degrees, the lectures belonging to each degree, and a description of the ceremony of each degree. He passed the examination, and when it was over an hour and a half had elapsed, the work in lodge had terminated, and the brethren were seated at the festive board.

"I wouldn't count too heavily on fraternal ties, Roger."

REMARKABLE MEMORY

An Eastern Star publication (of all places) is responsible for the following:

Three very small youngsters were bragging to each other about how far back they could remember.

"I can remember when I was only three years old," said one.

"I remember the day I started in Kindergarten," said the second boy.

The third member of the group smugly countered with:

"You two are pikers. I can remember the very day I was born; yes, I remember it very well, because nobody was there except me and my grandma. Mother and daddy had gone to an Eastern Star meeting."

BIGAMY

The letters on the circle around the keystone of a chapter of Royal Arch Masons has been paraphrased by some to "King Solomon had 20 wives, some say 30."

FAITH IN FOUR-LETTER WORDS

I would encourage my brother Masons to restore their faith in four-letter words.

Descriptive Saxon words offend us only briefly in life. And there are much more important four-letter words in the English language that guide us all through our years. For openers, let me suggest: Lord, Soul, Love, Work, Hope, Good, Free, Life.

You can think of others. Together they far outnumber and outweigh the unimportant four-letter words that try to compromise man's dignity but never make the grade.

(WALTER J. KLEIN—*The New Age*)

BUCK FEVER

It was the first meeting after installation. The junior deacon had just been advanced from senior steward. It was his first time to officiate in that place. To add to the feeling of buck fever, the district deputy was present. In closing the master asked regarding the duties of the tiler. He was told, "To guard against the approach of Evens and Cowsdroppers."

SHE KNEW THE ANSWERS

Sunday School Teacher:
"Who reigned after Saul?"
Little Bessie:
"David."
Teacher:
"And who came after David?"
Bessie:
"Solomon."
Teacher:
"And who came after Solomon?"
Bessie:
"The Queen of Sheba."

X

"A laugh is worth a hundred groans in any market."
(LAMB)

HARMONY PREVAILS

One of the regulations of Massachusetts' Bristol Lodge, which was established in 1797, was:

"No liquor shall be brought into the lodge, except by order of the Master. Fighting is forbidden during the opening, or within 30 minutes of the closing of the lodge."

MISSOURI'S FIRST

Grocery stores were questionable places in 1852 if we may believe this section of the by-laws of Sedalia, Missouri's first lodge:

Visiting a grocery store for the purpose of playing at cards, or any other game of chance, shall be found guilty of un-Masonic conduct.

And the lodge did a banking business among its members:

On motion, resolved that the W.M. in the absence of the treasurer be authorized to loan any money on hand belonging to the lodge and not needed for the expense of the lodge upon such terms as shall be conducive to the interest of the lodge.

In later records we find that a rate of 6 per cent was conducive to the interest of the lodge.

TOP CAT

We are told that the Prince Hall Affiliation sometimes refer to their Master as "The Cat with the hat."

WHAT SHALL WE DO WITH THE BODY?

A story that made the rounds a few years ago as "gospel truth" involved a Brother on a hunting trip in the wilds of Maine. Day after day of his vacation was eaten up without getting his deer. On the last day, as he was about to give up in desperation, he heard a crashing in the woods; saw a glimpse of brown and fired. Silence!

Rushing over to where he had fired, he found that he had killed a bull moose, which is protected from hunters to save it from extinction. As he stood there staring at the dead moose, a Game Warden stepped into the clearing. Our brother found his hands involuntarily raised in a certain position, "What shall we do with the body?"

"Dress it out, you damn fool," said the Warden, "and make your escape!

DONATION

We are indebted to R.W. Bro. Peter Rasmussen, that grand old man who fathered American Masonry in Germany and served as the first Provincial Grand Master of the American-Canadian Provincial Grand Lodge, within the United Grand Lodges of Germany, for the following story. "Brother Pete" frequently tells this story after an initiation as he reminisces.

Years ago, Wheaton (Illinois) Lodge used to meet in chambers over a hardware store. One cold winter night, the candidate was the proprietor of the hardware store. When the "demand" was made, he scratched his head, thought a minute, and said, "Well. You know last fall you boys got that new pot-bellied stove over there from me. You ain't never paid for it, so I'll donate it."

"Brother Pete" says that it was duly recorded that the merchant was then and there made a Mason.

JOINER

In Hutchinson, Kansas, Jeweler Glenn Brown caught a bad-check artist who casually remarked that he was both a member of the Knights of Columbus and the Masons.

(*Time,* December 8, 1952)

YOUR MARK

The Mark, or penny, is said to be the wages for good and faithful service. It has the value of 25 cents—or a Jewish half-shekel of silver. This at least is what we are taught in the MM degree. So! Let's look into the history of your mark or penny. The earliest specimens of coined shekels were issued about 144 B.C., prior to that time the shekel was a measure of weight. They generally showed a pot of manna with the inscription—SHEKEL ISRAEL— in old Samaritan characters on one side and on the other was the Rod of Aaron with three buds and the inscription—KADOSHAH—or "JERUSALEM the HOLY" in similar characters.

This design is found on quite a few marks used by the different chapters throughout the world. However note should be made that this is a FULL SHEKEL, not a half. In 1895 Comp. A. G. Pitts of King Cyrus Chapter No. 133 (in the grand State of) Michigan, chanced to see a full-shekel of the second year of the coinage of Simon Maccabaeus. Thinking the design approprate, he had a jeweler copy the reverse; then using a Keystone for the other side, Companion Pitts at last had a most impressive mark. Being highly pleased, he published a description in the February 1896 *The American Tyler,* in which he stated that a half-shekel was used. Thus was the beginning of the Mark as most of us know it today. You can't praise a man too highly for giving the craft something so wonderful, even if a small error was made.

CLEANUP

With the traditional German cry of "Feierabend" the Junior Warden announces the end of the day. The last 20 minutes are spent by all members of the lodge in cleaning up the collation room and assisting the Stewards.

(From the *Trestleboard* of Schleissheim Lodge No. 878, Munich, Germany)

THE SHORTEST EXAMINATION

A Brother from Colorado went to England on a month's vacation. While there, he tried his very best to get an invitation to an English Masonic Lodge, but to no avail. Finally, on the eve of the day of his departure for home he was out with an English acquaintance and suggested that they might go out together to celebrate. "No" the English friend said, "I have to go to a meeting of my Masonic Lodge." The American then confessed to the fact that he had tried to get invited to an English Lodge, but without results. The Briton hesitated, then asked him if he were willing to take an examination. The American replied that he would be glad to undergo one. The Englishman thought for a moment and then queried, "What did you see when you first entered a Masonic Lodge?" The American replied, "Nothing. I was hoodwinked and could not see a thing." With that the Englishman said, "Come along. You're a Mason, all right."

A PERCIFENT FOR THE ZOO

Under a flaring headline "High State Mason Here" the *Kansas City Star* of May 26, 1947, tells of the visit of the Grand Master; in listing guests, we find:

"F. Ernest Carter, grand percifent."

Thus are new and strange jobs created in the Grand Lodge of Missouri.

SHORT CUT?

Mispronounced words have plagued ritualists for years, but consider the dismay of a Senior Deacon who instead of "circumscribing desires" managed to have them "circumsized."

CHARITY SUFFERETH NOT

Here's another version of a common story: One day the priest of Pat's Parish encountered him on the street. The priest berated Pat for not attending Mass, but Pat told him that he was out of work and his clothing hardly fit for use, and that he could use $80 to make himself presentable to look for new work. The priest told Pat that he couldn't help him financially, but for Pat to have hope and pray. Pat wrote a letter, addressed to God, telling Him of his straits, and dropped it in the nearest mailbox. The mail clerk found it while sorting, and placed the letter on the postmaster's desk. The postmaster who was a Mason took the letter to lodge, where the matter was discussed, but since Pat was not a Mason they could not use any of the Lodge funds. However, they took up a collection, amounting to $50, and mailed it to Pat in an envelope bearing the lodge return address. Shortly after that the priest and Pat met once again. Pat had purchased new clothes with the money, and looked quite spruce. Pat told the priest that his prayer had been answered, but that he hoped God wouldn't use the Masons again, as they had kept nearly half of the money needed!

A LONG CABLETOW

Albert Pike Lodge in Utah, desired to add a section to its bylaws providing that no loans could be made by the lodge "to a member, or to a member's father, mother, wife, son, daughter, sister, brother, uncle, aunt, nephew, niece, first cousin, mother-in-law, father-in-law, sister-in-law, brother-in-law, son-in-law, or daughter-in-law." The Grand Master thought there was nothing objectionable to the amendment and if the lodge chose to do so they could, so long as they did not entirely exhaust a man's family tree.

THE SIGN OF A FREEMASON

The ill-disguised curiosity of the cowan appears to have been a never-failing source of amusement to our brethren of the last century. . . . A Quaker Mason formed one of an indiscriminate company of cowans at an inn, where the landlord was also a brother. Numerous jokes were cracked at the expense of the Fraternity, and the Quaker was called upon to show them the Mason's sign. One of the company offered to give him a bottle of wine if he would comply with their wishes; and, at length, though with much apparent reluctance, he agreed, on condition that the wine should be immediately produced, and the individual consented to receive the communication privately; the Quaker adding: "Friend, if thou does not confess to the company that I have shown thee a Freemason's sign, I will pay for the wine myself." The proposition was too reasonable to be refused, and the curious candidate for Masonic knowledge retired into another room with his formal friend. When there, the following dialogue took place:

Quaker: "So, friend, thou are desirous of seeing a Freemason's sign?"

Cowan: "I am."

Quaker: "Canst thou keep a secret?"

Cowan: "Try me."

Quaker: "Good! Thou knowest that our friend Johnson (the inn keeper) is a Mason?"

Cowan: "I do."

Quaker: "Very well." Then taking him by the arm, he led him to the window. "Dost thou see that ramping lion which swings from yonder upright post?"

Cowan: "To be sure I do—it is our landlord's sign."

Quaker: "Good! Then friend, our landlord being a Freemason, thou art satisfied that I have shown thee a Freemason's sign, and thy bottle of wine is forfeited. For thy own sake, thou wilt keep the secret."

The cowan returned into the room with a look of astonishment, confessing that he had received the desired information; and the mystery, which he purposely observed, tempted others to purchase the secret at the same price.

(*Iowa Grand Lodge Bulletin,* October 1941)

SACRIFICE

It was the night to receive the Master Mason degree. The veterinarian was all "dolled up" and ready to go, when he received a telephone call to come and castrate a farmer's hog. He demurred, but was told that if he didn't come that night, the farmer would take his business elsewhere. Finally he went, dressed in his very best, and did the job. It was getting late—the veterinarian was in a hurry—so he wrapped up the parts removed—shoved them in his coat pocket, and hurried to the lodge. He was selected to be the first candidate, and as he was preparing to go into the lodgeroom, he thought of what was in his coat pocket, and hurled the package through the transom. When they came back for the other candidates, all had left!

"At this time I would like to place in nomination for high priest the following name . . ."

DESIDERATA

- Go placidly amid the noise and haste,
- And remember what peace there may be in silence.
- As far as possible without surrender be on good terms with all persons.
- Speak your truth quietly and clearly; and listen to others; even the dull and ignorant; they too have their story.
- Avoid loud and aggressive persons, they are vexations to the spirit.
- If you compare yourself with others, you may become vain and bitter; for always there will be greater and lesser persons than yourself. Enjoy your achievements as well as your plans.
- Keep interested in your own career, however humble; it is a real possession in the changing fortunes of time. Exercise caution in your business affairs; for the world is full of trickery. But let

this not blind you to what virtue there is; many persons strive for high ideals; and everywhere life is full of heroism.

- Be yourself. Especially, do not feign affection. Neither be cynical about love; for in the face of all aridity and disenchantment, it is perennial as the grass.
- Take kindly the counsel of years, gracefully surrendering the things of youth. Nurture strength of spirit to shield you in sudden misfortune. But do not distress yourself with imaginings. Many fears are born of fatigue and loneliness. Beyond a wholesome discipline, be gentle with yourself.
- You are a child of the universe, no less than the trees and the stars; you have a right to be here. And whether or not it is clear to you, no doubt the universe is unfolding as it should.
- Be therefore at peace with God, whatever you conceive him to be, and whatever your labors and aspirations in the noisy confusion of life, keep peace with your soul.
- With all its sham, drudgery and broken dreams, it is still a beautiful world. Be careful. Strive to be happy.

(Found in old Saint Pauls Church, Baltimore. Dated 1692.
Submitted by Brother John Roope Rasquin)

DON'T GET MIXED UP WITH THAT CROWD

From the Virginia proceedings, which always has a lot of good stories, we take one told by George Bushnell, of Michigan. The judge was describing an old harness maker in a Virginia town in which he was born and raised; he was Uncle Hershey Carper:

"No one matched Uncle Hershey. He was as careful and as cautious as he could be. I remember I came home one time and he said:

" 'What's that I hear about a lodge in Detroit with over 5,000 members?'

"I said: 'That's right, Uncle Hershey.'

"He said: 'I don't care anything about what you say about its being right, it's clandestine to me, so you stay away from it.'

"And he said: 'I don't believe it because they couldn't get 5,000 members without soliciting some of them, so you keep away from that crowd. We don't want you mixed up with them.' "

SYMBOLS

Symbols have meaning only in terms of experience. Since no two men's experiences are ever exactly the same, they often give different interpretation to the same symbols. A good illustration of this is the different meaning attached to the symbols of sound heard by four travelers in the compartment of a European train—a colonel, a sergeant, an old maid, and her attractive niece.

As the train entered a tunnel there was the sound of a kiss followed by the sound of a slap. Each properly identified the symbols but not two gave the same meaning to them. The maiden aunt thought the sergeant had kissed her niece and been slapped for his efforts. The niece thought the colonel had kissed her aunt and that she had slapped him. The colonel knew he had been slapped. He figured the sergeant had kissed the young lady; she had thought he —the colonel—had done it and had slapped him. Only the sergeant had enough experience with what had happened to give proper interpretation to what he heard. He knew that he had kissed the back of his hand and then slapped the colonel.

(GLEN S. FAXON, SR.)

STORY WITH MORAL

A Mason was hunting in the forest. A terrible storm came up. He looked for shelter but there was none. It was raining in torrents so he crawled into a hollow log. It fitted snugly. The rain lasted for hours and the water soaked through the wood. The log began to contract. The storm abated and the man tried to get out, but could not. He strained but to no avail. The log held him tight. He knew he would die of starvation unless he could free himself. His whole life flashed before him, especially his mistakes. Suddenly he remembered he had not paid his lodge dues. This made him feel SO SMALL that he was able to crawl out of the log. The moral of this story is: Do not let your dues accumulate until you are in a tight pinch.

GETTING HIS ATTENTION

A member of a Texas degree team was criticized for resorting to unnecessary roughness at the East Gate in the second section of the Master Mason degree.

His reply: "Before I could impress him with the solemnity of the occasion, I had to first get his attention."

CANDIDATE

It may not be termed "humor" because of its seriousness, yet there is a certain element of humor in an announcement which we ran across. Names and places are purposely omitted.

Dear Brother: This is to announce that I expect to be a candidate for ——— at the coming communication of the Grand Lodge. It is needless to say that I have held all the subordinate offices that candidates for ——— have usually held. I could give the usual reasons why I should be given the office but they are rather trite. The real reason is of course that I want the "job." If you are not already pledged to another candidate, I would appreciate receiving your vote.

Fraternally

. . . .

On the back of the card, which was distributed on the floor of the grand lodge, were the Masonic records of the "candidate," which included

Star: Patron four or five times
Treasurer Fireman's Association
State Rural Letter Carriers' Association

Note: He was *not* elected.

NOT QUITE RIGHT

Stewart Pollard, author-compiler of this Volume is a Sergeant Major in the U.S. Army. The Army abbreviation for this rank is "SGM." Imagine his surprise when he was introduced in a small Massachusetts lodge by a Brother with whom he had been corresponding, as "Sovereign Grand Master."

THE PSALM

The Active member of the Craft is my shepherd. I shall not want.

He provideth me with privileges and benefits of the Craft, so that I may lie down in green pastures, beside the still waters.

He restoreth prosperity in the Craft.

He guideth the welfare of the Craft without any contribution made by me, I stray in the paths of unrighteous for my plèasure's sake.

Yea, though I alibi, and do not attend meeting after meeting, I fear no evil, for he is active and protects the Craft for me.

The petitions and work for new members, which he provides—comforts me.

He prepareth a table before me—called a Banquet—in the presence of all who would condemn me, by his own labors.

He anointeth my head with oil of Faith, Brotherly Love and Relief. And my cup runneth over, Love ingratitude.

Surely, his goodness and loving kindness shall follow me all the days of my life—without any cooperation from me.

I shall dwell in his house forever, and allow him to work, and work, and work for me—the Nonactive Member of the Craft.

(Florida York Rite Light)

HIS AFTER DINNER SPEECH

"Kind friends," your praise I don't deserve. I feel, I feel – ahem – I feel the night is growing short. I've said more than I really ought. The time is not afforded me to speak at length tonight. I thank you," - then sat down -

And everyone applauded.

SOME OLD MASONIC TOASTS

To the brother who stands plumb to his principles, yet is level to his brethren

May the altitude of our virtues ever be at high twelve.

To each faithful brother, both ancient and young,
Who governs his passions and bridles his tongue.

May we correct our own faults before we publish those of our brothers.

XI

"An ounce of cheerfulness is worth a pound of sadness to serve God with."

(FULLER)

NEWS OF THE CONGREGATION

A news letter published by the First Christian Church of North Kansas City, Missouri, contained this item about two members of the congregation:

"Our congratulations to Fred Neuswanger and Harry Palmitier, who were initiated into the 32nd degree of Freemasonry in the York Rite this past weekend."

The good brothers had, in fact, been members of the class taking all of the York Rite degrees in a fall festival at nearby Independence, Missouri.

DON'T DO NOTHIN'

A distinguished and scholarly Missouri Past Grand Master recalls during his term of office a letter from a rural lodge asking "can you come and visit our lodge? We meet on the first Saturday after the full moon."

The Grand Master finally located a calendar that showed the phases of the moon and replied to the lodge that he could visit and what did they want him to do?

The reply came quickly:

"We're glad you can come.

"We don't want you to do nothing.

"We got a full program.

"We just want to see you!"

The Grand Master said he went, they did have a full program, and, they did just want to see him.

(M.W. BRO. HAROLD O. GRAUEL—Missouri)

HAPPINESS, ANYONE?

This is a résumé of the preliminary findings of two scientists: a psychiatrist and a physiologist. Their report covers a period of over

20 years of observation and experiments, from their personal experiences and those of their colleagues. It is not certain that they are Masons, but the figures known and divulged are strangely revealing.

The happiness cycle is 33 days and the happiness period lasts from three minutes to three days.

The happiness period comes once in 33 days and its duration, varying in length in persons, is characterized by an inner and/or outer glow in them, noticeable specially in their physiognomy, particularly their eyes. There is spring and lilt in their actions, quite discernible in their posture, particularly when they walk. Their speech during the period is positive, hopeful, romantic; does not have any trace of the negative, critical, condemnatory.

During the rest of the cycle, depressive moments are common especially among the introverts; but, with the extroverts, acting out happiness is common. Many people can turn a blue situation into a rosy one.

(*Cabletow*)

SQUELCHED TEXAN

A Texas brother was visiting a small lodge in Vermont. Between sections of the degree work, he struck up a conversation with the brother seated next to him. In the conversation, the Texan inquired the extent of the Vermonter's farm acreage. The answer was 180 acres. The Texan replied, "Back in Texas I get into my Cadillac, drive all day before I can reach the other end of my acreage." The Vermonter replied, "Yup! I had a car like that once. I sold it!"

THOUGHTS FOR THINKERS

What we get without effort, is more of a curse than a blessing. What we get out of Masonry is no exception to the rule.

* * *

It is a sad fact that there are few reading Masons—that is those who read about Masonry. Why is this? Mostly because the average Masonic writer writes too much, and says too little.

THE SECRETARY'S REWARD

The Secretary stood at the pearly gate,
His face was worn and old;
He merely asked the man at the gate
For admission to the fold.

"What did you do down there?," St. Peter asked,
"To gain admission here?"
"Oh, I used to be a Secretary
Down there for many a year."

The pearly gate swung open sharp
As St. Peter tapped the bell.
"Come in, Old Top, and take your harp;
You had enough of hell!"

TONIGHT I RAISE MY SON

My son is to become a Master Mason tonight, and to me is given the honor of raising him.

I am sitting in my big chair before the fireplace. The family has gone out, and, as I have watched the flames curl up the chimney, I have sat back in retrospection, and before my eyes have passed all of the eventful happenings of my life.

How well I remembered the day he came to us, and how happy we all were. He was just a wee, tiny bundle of humanity, but within his little body were confined all the hopes and happiness and dreams of a devoted father and a devoted mother who had made almost the supreme sacrifice that he might live.

There comes to me today a little poem which I copied many years ago. I have forgotten the author:

Thee, on thy mother's knee, a
New-born babe in tears we found,
While all about thee smiled.

"So live that, sinking in thy last
Long sleep, smiles may be thine
While all about thee weep."

As he grew up, how his mother had planned and saved for each stage of his development. We wanted him to have all of the advantages which we had.

These were happy years—years of sacrifice cheerfully made that he might have all of the advantages. But the sacrifices were more than compensated for by the love and respect which he gave us both. As he developed into manhood he seemed to glow with the love and fire and ambition of youth.

There are several events that stand out in my life, but none more poignantly than the day he came to me and said: "Dad, I would like to join the Masons; will you take my application?"

And so, tonight, he is to become a Master Mason, and I am to raise him. Am I worthy? Dear God, give me the strength and ability to so impress him with the teachings of Freemasonry that for its precepts and principles as I have done.

More than this I shall not ask.

(*The Key*)

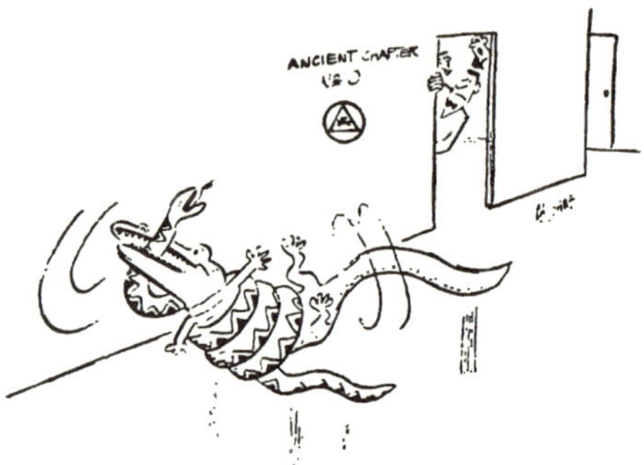

"Don, must you interrupt the Chapter meeting for every little thing that goes on out in the hall?"

LOOK IN THE MIRROR

Since the general tone of any organization reflects the sum of the members comprising it, the condition of Freemasonry, and of your lodge in particular, holds up the mirror to you. . . . How do you look? Handsome, of course, but are you eager to combat the competition facing our Fraternity today?

(*British Columbia Masonic Bulletin*)

THE SECRETS OF FREEMASONRY

Our story concerns the doings of an Ozark lodge of more than a century ago; since the personnel of the story have been long deceased they would not be embarrassed by our story—BUT some of their descendants might—hence no names.

This certain lodge was located in a backwoods area where things were wild and sometimes woolly. The meeting place was in the only two-story building in miles thereabouts; beneath was a saloon (this was in the days when grand lodge overlooked a lodge's surroundings).

One of the better element complained to the grand master.

He said in his complaint that the lodge room was above a saloon;

that there were planks in the floor which were loose and which stuck up endangering lives of candidates and members; that the window lights had been knocked out and that people below could hear the secrets of Freemasonry as they were being communicated.

The master did not show up at grand lodge when the complaint was being heard, but there was a sole representative. He was asked as to the truth of the situation; he did not dispute the facts, but he did offer (what he thought to be) a satisfactory explanation.

It is true that we do meet upstairs over a saloon, but this is the only safe (?) place for the meeting of a lodge in a hundred miles; and the master of the lodge is the proprietor of the saloon and the only one at all capable of conferring in his own way the degrees of Freemasonry.

It is also true that boards are loose in the floor, but most of the members know where they are—and they do afford a convenient spot for those who chew, to spit, for we have no spittoons.

And as for the window lights being out, this is also true, for we are financially unable to replace them; there is no glass in our village—and as for people below hearing the secrets of Freemasonry —I have been a member of that lodge for 30 years—and if they ever had any secrets, I have yet to hear them!

(*The Royal Arch Mason*)

MIRROR, MIRROR, ON THE WALL

A rich man visited a clergyman who took him by the arm and led him to a window.

"Look out there," said the clergyman. The rich man looked out into the street. "What do you see?" asked the clergyman.

"People," answered the rich man. Again the clergyman took his visitor by the arm and led him to a mirror.

"What do you see now?" asked the clergyman.

The rich man replied, "Now I see *myself*."

The clergyman then observed: "Behold, in the window there is glass and in the mirror there is glass. But the mirror glass is backed by silver. And no sooner is the silver added than we cease to see others and only see ourselves."

(Anonymous)

BUILDING

I watched them tearing a building down
A gang of men in a busy town

With a yo-heave-ho and lusty yell,
They swung a beam and the side wall fell.

I asked the foreman: "Are these men skilled—
The kind you would hire if you wanted to build?"
He laughed and said: "Why, no, indeed,
Just common labor is all I need;
They can easily wreck in a day or two
What builders have taken years to do."

I asked myself, as I went my way,
Which of these roles have I tried today?
Am I a builder who works with care,
Measuring life by the rule and square,
Shaping my deeds by the well-made plan,
Patiently doing the best I can?
Or am I a wrecker who walks the town,
Content with the labor of tearing down?
(Author Unknown)

THE MASONIC WAY

To go about your work with pleasure, to greet others with a word of encouragement, to be happy in the present and confident in the future; this is to have achieved some measure of success in living.
(EDWIN OSGOOD GROVER)

"That reminds me . . . isn't your lodge dinner tonight?"

"Say! That was a good hole-in-one . . . but to continue with this project our Royal Arch Chapter has in mind. . . ."

KNIFE AND FORK DEGREE

I do not attend the meetings
for I've not the time to spare.
But every time they have a feast
You'll surely find me there.
I cannot help with the degrees
for I do not know the work.
But I can applaud the speaker
and handle the knife and fork.
I am so rusty in the ritual that
it seems like Greek to me.
But practice makes me perfect
in the knife and fork degree.

TEMPERED HUMOR

A sense of humor is what makes you laugh at something which would make you mad, if it happened to you.

MASONRY SPEAKS TO THE NEW MASON

You have tonight become a Master Mason.

I have given you all that I can give in ritual, lectures and symbolism. What I give you from this point on will depend upon your willingness to sacrifice, to work and to learn. . . .

In your work or profession you may attain great success. But the greatest satisfaction you will have in life will come from the living of my principles and teachings. If you strive diligently, I will show the way to the greatest of all wisdom, the path that leads to the knowledge of self.

If you attend my meetings regularly; if you will make me a vital part of your life; if you learn and share what you learn with your Brothers, you will discover the secret of happiness.

If you use my Working Tools wisely, you will build a Temple that will defy the onslaught of time.

Into your hands tonight I have placed our age-old secrets, our honored traditions, our sacred heritage.

All of this I do with complete confidence that you will think, act, and live as a Master Mason.

(DEWEY H. WOLLSTEIN, *Masonic Messenger*)

"I'm afraid our electing Charlie to High Priest has gone to his head."

A PLUG FOR SHORTER MEETINGS

Blessed are they who have nothing to say, and who cannot be persuaded to say it.

MISTAKES

When a plumber makes a mistake, he charges twice for it.

When a lawyer makes a mistake, he has a chance to try the case again.

When a doctor makes a mistake, he buries it.

When a judge makes a mistake, it becomes the law of the land.

When a preacher makes a mistake, nobody knows the difference.

But, if during a Masonic degree, a member of the ritual team, an electrician or property-man makes an error—GOOD NIGHT.

IF I DON'T GO, I DON'T GET

One of the most profound gems of philosophy especially applicable to Freemasonry that I have ever heard, came from an old man in the South who lived in a small house on the bank of a wide river.

His only income was from ferrying passengers across the river in a row boat. It was hard work. His hands were calloused by constant labor at the oars. His face was tanned and weatherbeaten. But it was the kindly face of one who had spent much time contemplating the wonders of nature and pondering on things of the spirit.

"How many times do you go across the river in a day?" asked a passenger. The reply was: "I go as often as I can. The more I go, the more I get. If I don't go, I don't get."

What an inspiration in regard to lodge attendance is to be found in those simple words. I wish that every Mason could read and would take to his heart this sublime bit of homespun philosophy.

(ROBERT G. COLE)

TEMPLE OF LIVING STONES

What honored names on history's page,
O'er whose brave deeds we pore,
Have knelt before our Sacred Shrine
And trod our "checkered floor."

Kings, princes, statesmen, heroes,
Bards who square their actions true,
Between the pillars of the porch,
Now pass in long review:

O, Brothers, what a glorious thought
For us to dwell upon,—
The Mystic Tie that binds our hearts
Bound that of Washington!

Although our past achievements we
With honest pride review,
As long as there's rough ashlars,
There is work for us to do:

We must shape the living stones with
Instruments of love
For that eternal mansion in the
Paradise above:

Toil as we've toiled in ages past
To carry out the plan,—
'Tis this:—the Fatherhood of God,
The Brotherhood of man.

(LAWRENCE N. GREENLEAF)

THE ORIGINAL

Whatever troubles Adam had,
No man in days of yore
Could say, when Adam cracked a joke,
"I've heard that one before."

ELECTRIFYING

Reporting on the experience of guiding a group of Job's Daughters on a tour in Washington, the Matron of the Star Chapter reported that the girls were "real live wires." A soft male voice on the sidelines was heard to say: "No wonder they're live wires, they carry practically no insulation." (Which reminds us of the Chairman of the Lodge Budget Committee who explained that his statistics were like Bikini bathing suits—what they reveal is important, but what they conceal is vital.)

WHAT YOU SHOULD LEARN

There are five things in life which everyone ought to learn:

1. Learn to laugh. A good laugh is better than medicine. When you smile or laugh, your brain for the moment is freed from the load that it ordinarily carries.

2. Learn to tell a helpful story. A well-told story is as wholesome and welcome as a sunbeam in a sick room.

3. Learn to keep your troubles to yourself. The world is too busy to linger over your ills and sorrows.

4. Learn to stop croaking. If you cannot see any good in this world, keep the bad to yourself.

5. Learn to greet your friends with a smile. They carry too many frowns in their own hearts to be bothered with any of yours.

(Borrowed)

FOR THOSE WHO COME AFTER ME

A newly raised brother attending his first meeting of Blue Lodge saw a rather aged Mason sitting in the Senior Deacon chair. When the lodge was called from labor to refreshment, he approached the chair, and said, "Why are you sitting in that chair? Surely you don't expect to live long enough to 'reach the East'?" Upon which the "old master" replied, "The word is 'sit,' brother, and I will tell you a little story.

"My ancestors planted acorns, I doubt if they ever expected to see the oak trees, but they planted them for their children to sit in the shade and enjoy the fruits of their labor.

"I do likewise in the lodge for those who will come after me. I believe it is time to get back to labor."

(A. P. BERNHARDT)

WHAT KIND OF A MASON ARE YOU?

A lot of Masons are like wheelbarrows—no good unless pushed.
Some are like trailers—they have to be pulled.
Some are like kites—if you don't keep a string on them they fly away.
Some are like balloons—full of wind and ready to blow up.
Some are like footballs—you can't tell which way they will bounce.
And then, some are like a good watch—open face, pure gold, quietly busy, and full of good works.

OTHERS OR SELF

The Mason who is not willing to forego his own pleasure to add to those of his brethren, is either too dull to learn its teachings, or too selfish to put them into practice.

(WOR. E. A. MCHAN—Georgia)

A NIGHT OF WONDERING

M.W. Bro. Albert P. Rue'Rat, Past Grand Master of the Grand Lodge of Rhode Island and Past Grand Master of the Order of DeMolay told this story at the Grand Lodge of Maine.

Despite everything man is a very ingenious person and I think I can best describe it by borrowing a story from that great Masonic leader and civic leader of Kansas City, Missouri, Mayor H. Roe Bartle who happens to tell the story of a Masonic Grand Lodge meeting in Kansas City not too many years ago where three prominent members of the Grand Lodge were housed in one of the better hotels of that city, and just for lack of proper identity let's call them Brothers Tom, Dick and Harry.

The following morning after their first night as guests of this hotel Harry saw Tom in the lobby and Tom was one of the most haggard Master Masons that one could ever expect to meet anywhere. Harry said, "Tom, you look awful! What's the matter with you?" Tom said, "Harry, I never put in such a night in my life. You see we were assigned a twin-bedded room. That is, when I say we, I am talking about Dick and myself; and I suppose that you have a sleeping companion, too." Harry said, "No, I was fortunate enough to have a double single bed for me." Tom said, "Harry, you are pretty lucky because that guy Dick can snore and snore and snore. I didn't sleep a wink all night long." Harry said, "Now look, Tom, don't let that bother you. You swap rooms with me tonight. I would just as soon sleep in the same room with Dick and that doesn't bother me a bit." Tom said, "Oh I wouldn't have you make that sacrifice." Harry replied, "Look, we .are all members of the same Fraternity and Brothers and this is one thing I can do for you." Sure enough, they agreed.

The next morning when Tom met Harry in the lobby, Harry was a bright eyed and bushy tailed as could be and he said, "Harry, you don't mean to tell me you could sleep with that guy Dick snoring all night?" Harry said, "I had no problems. Dick took his shower, got into his P.J.'s and got into bed. I took my shower and got into my P.J.'s and went over and kissed him goodnight and he stayed awake all night wondering what was going to happen."

* * *

(The following poem written by Milford Shields, P.M., Poet Laureate, was inspired by the Aprons at the Masonic Grand Lodge Session held in Denver on January 28-29, 1969.)

THE APRON

I took an apron from the pile of white
And tied it on to sit in Lodge one night.
As I sat there I felt a warming glow
About the apron and I looked and lo—
The other brethren who had worn it there
Were gathered 'round in mystic meeting rare.

We shared with each the blessings of the years,
The dreams, successes, hopes and joyous tears;
Then we grew humble in each other's loss,
In full compassion shared each brother's cross;
Our hearts were one in that most holy place,
Our spirits fused in God's Masonic grace.

We looked upon the apron's perfect white,
We all were wearing it that mystic night,
We saw that it was large enough to fit
The whole wide world, for God had fashioned it.

"Let .ne have another look at those tickets."

BACKGROUND

One of the joys of compiling this volume has been the extensive correspondence with brethren from all over the world which it has caused. In one letter—from M.W. Bro. Clarence H. Cohen, Past Grand Master of the Grand Lodge of Georgia—casual mention was made of a book with an intriguing title—*Masonic Stories; Things Masons Ought to Know; Things and Other Things,* written by Wor. Bro. Edgar Allen McHan and published in 1922.

The search for a copy began! There just might be some humor in a book with that title! There wasn't a copy of it in the Grand Lodge Library of the Grand Lodge of the District of Columbia. After an extensive search, the ever-helpful gal who works in the Masonic Service Association regretfully informed me that she couldn't find a copy in their library. At the Library of Congress I not only drew a "blank," but also a "you've-got-to-be-kidding" look. R.W. Earle D. Webster, Grand Secretary of the Grand Lodge of Maine, who maintains their excellent Masonic Library also expressed regrets.

This gave me an excuse to put in a long distance call to my old friend, Wor. Bro. Walter M. Callaway, Jr., who recently took over the reins as Editor and Business Manager of the *Masonic Messenger,* the excellent magazine of the Grand Lodge of Georgia. That was somewhat of a mistake! Between his eagerness to talk—and the slowness of his Southern drawl—it was an expensive call. However, it brought results!

Two days later, I received a letter from Brother Callaway which put me on the right track. The Grand Chapter (RAM) Library of Georgia did indeed have a copy, and the Grand Secretary, M.E. Comp. J. E. Mosely, most graciously loaned it to this Yankee Companion.

Written in the turn-of-the-century style, *Masonic Stories, Things Masons Ought to Know, Things and Other Things* is indeed worth the time and effort expended to get it.

Under the chapter heading "War Time Stories," Wor. Brother McHan related the following two accounts of Masonry in action.

* * *

In the little city of Canton, nestling among the hills of Cherokee County, there is one of those beautiful before-the-war homes, which stands today as a monument of the power of the square and compasses.

If you will take the trouble to examine the house, you will find it bears scars made by the incendiary's torch, and the old people will tell you that this was the only house left in this proud little city after Sherman made his well-remembered trip through Georgia.

I was told this story by one who was born and reared in the house. He told me that when the Army came into Canton, burning everything before it, that this house was fired with the rest. There was of course no man about the place to help extinguish the fire, and his mother and the children drew water from the well and succeeded in putting it out. This they did three different times. The fourth time the incendiaries determined to succeed, so after firing the house, they cut the well rope and removed it.

You can imagine the feelings of this mother, as she saw the fire eating its way into her beautiful home, and realizing the hopelessness of saving anything.

Suddenly in her dire distress, a thought came to her, and like the drowning man who grasps at even a straw, she immediately acted upon the impulse. Rushing into the house and opening a drawer, she took therefrom a Mason's apron, bearing upon its pure white surface, the emblems of the order. Armed with this apron alone, she rushed from the burning building in search of someone in charge of the soldiers. Seeing a man whom she judged to be an officer, she approached him, and holding the apron before his face, demanded to know if he was a Mason, and if so, that he should save her home.

Without answering her question by word of mouth, he ordered the men under his command to extinguish the flame at once.

After the fire was put out, the officer placed a guard near the house, with orders to see that no one should damage the property, or in any manner disturb the inmates of the home.

It is not at all strange that the impressions made upon the mind of the youth in his home should have influenced him to seek admission among members of the Fraternity, as soon as he should become man, and it was he who related this story in the presence of a number of brethren who are subscribers to the *Herald,* and who will verify what I have written to be substantially what he told us.

* * *

Captain H ————, a veteran of the civil war, who related to me this story which I am sure has never been published before, is still living in Clayton County, and the last time I saw him, was hale and hearty.

The Captain was captured, I think he said, in Virginia, something like a year before the close of the war, and was placed in prison, where he was forced to remain until the surrender, except as hereinafter related.

To start with, the Captain is one of the most lovable characters it has ever been my privilege to know. He is a gentleman of the old school and the very soul of honor.

Soon after being placed in prison, there was a mutual discovery made by himself and the officer in charge, and while one wore the blue and the other the gray, and while one was the captor and the other the prisoner, yet they learned they were brother Masons. The Captain says he did not mention Masonry to the officer, nor did he mention it to him, still he could not fail to note, and other prisoners noted it also, that he was given more liberties and treated with greater respect than the others.

He had been confined several months as a prisoner, and during the entire time had been treated by the officer as an equal, when one day he received a message from home that one of his family was very sick and would probably not live but a short time. The Captain said that when he received this information, his heart sank within him, and he felt tempted to give the sign of distress to his captor, and plead to be permitted to escape; but remembering how kindly he had been treated, he felt that it would be really dishonorable to do such a thing, and he determined to bear his burden like a soldier. The officer at once saw that some great sorrow had come to his prisoner, and brother-like, he inquired to know what the trouble was.

His interest was so brotherly and sympathetic, that he at once overcame the Captain's quiet dignity, and he told him the news he had just received from home. Without a moment's hesitancy the officer asked him if he would like to go home.

"I certainly would," was his reply.

"If I allow you to go home," said the officer, "Will you give me your word of honor as a Mason, that you will return?"

"I certainly will," said Captain H——————, "and I will return, if I live, you won't want me if I am dead."

"Then go," said the officer, "and I will supply your needs. I pray you may find the health of your loved one improved. Go, and come back soon as you can."

The Captain went home and no doubt his presence, and the kindly act of his captor in permitting him to see his loved one, had much to do with a speedy recovery.

A few weeks later, one evening, the other prisoners were surprised to see Captain H———— apply for admission into the prison enclosure, but the officer of the day exhibited no surprise, but greeted him kindly.

If we only knew of them, there have probably been many similar cases to this, but no matter how many there might be, each one only adds lustre to the beauty of the others.

MY BALLOT

I stand at the same sacred altar
  Where, prompted by brotherly love,
I vowed solemn vows without falter,
  Witnessed by Him from above.
As once I knelt there in rev'rence,
  I now stand rev'rently there—
My thoughts have suffered no sev'rance,
  As I vowed—so I'll vote—on the square.

If through friendship I favor the seeker
  But think him unworthy at heart—
Lest my Lodge by my ballot grow weaker,
  Such favor from justice must part.
At the altar where light flooded o'er me,
  I'll betray not the trust that I bear,
I'll shame not the emblems before me,
  But I'll cast that vote on the square.

Or should he not be to my liking,
  But merit by action the trust;
My soul I'll not perjure by striking
  A blow when such blow be unjust—
But I'll welcome his step 'cross the border,
  I'll honor the trust that I bear,
I'll vote for the good of the order
  By casting that vote on the square.

Time flies—and ere long my petition
  Will be filed in the Grand Lodge above.
I'll be glad then I tempered such mission
  With justice and brotherly love.
"With the measure ye mete" has been spoken
  By the Worshipful Master up there—
No promise e'er made has He broken
  And He'll handle my case on the square.

Yours for service,
THOMAS Q. ELLIS, Grand Master, 1925—Mississippi

XII

"How much lies in laughter: the cipher key, wherewith we decipher the whole man!"

(CARLYLE)

SICKNESS AND DISTRESS

A Mason wanted to move his membership from his home lodge to another lodge across town, so he got a dimit and presented it to the other lodge for consideration.

The investigating committee asked him his reason for the move. He told them he wanted it for health reasons. They told him they did not understand, that it was very unusual to move a membership for that reason.

His answer was they had *got sick of him* in his home lodge.

MY FIRST VISIT TO THE LODGE

It was three weeks ago that I became a member of Deep Hollow Lodge No. 111. That night I was so mixed up about what's happened, that I decided to go to the meeting tonight to see just how things are done there.

I got through with the milking early, fed the hens, saw that my pigs were penned up; then went to shave and again put on my blue suit that Uncle Dan gave me for confirmation, cranked up old Henry and started on the 29 mile trip to the lodge.

Little while after I got there the men all came in, sat down on the benches and looked kind of quiet. Then a feller at the end of the room sitting a bit higher than me, wearing a high hat, hit a hammer on something, said that everybody should watch how they're clothed. I knew he meant me, so I fixed my tie and took off my rubbers. Seems he must be the boss of the outfit because he gave orders to a lot of the men. There was a Father and Son there who had something to do with it. I know one was the junior and the other the senior, I can't remember their first names, but I think the last name was Warden.

Then along comes a fellar with a long stick in his hand, he shook hands with everybody, then they would stand up and blow in his ear, when he got to see me I shook hands and blew in his ear too, but he didn't like it much, he called me Confusion. Then the fellar, I think they called him the mister, asked if anyone knew me and they did, so that was alright. After that an old man got up and said some nice prayers and we all sang a song which was pretty good.

While we was still standing everybody starts moving their hands in different ways, so I did the same. Then along came a fellar, guess he belongs to the church, 'cause I heard them call him Deacon. He lit some candles. Can't figure why he did it because it was plenty light in the room then. Then the Mister told someone to tell the fellar outside that the lodge was open, but he didn't seem to care 'cause he didn't come in anyway.

Then the boss called the fellar at the desk Secretary and told him to do some reading, this was the first time I saw a real Secretary. I once seen a story in a magazine where a married man ran away with his Secretary. Couldn't imagine who would run away with that old man and what for.

The Mister got up and said the lodge was open and that he was looking for business. Don't think anybody gave him any, though a few of the men did some tall talking, a bit about sickness and other things. After a while the Mister told the Son of the Father that we were to have some refreshments. I waited around a bit to see what we would get to eat and drink, but seems they plumb forgot about it all, cause I didn't see nobody get anything so I got me my hat and coat and went home. Guess I won't go there anymore cause everybody's all mixed up jest like myself.

UNDUE ROUGHNESS

For more than 25 years, when Past Grand Master Ralph Pollard of Maine attended lodge, it was necessary for him to travel on a cot in an ambulance. Kindly brethren would carry him from the ambulance to the lodge room. One night, after a lodge meeting, as he was being carried to the ambulance, a young fellow standing on the street corner said to his buddy, "Gawd! That must've been *some* initiation them Masons had tonight."

MY CREED

Ten thousand paths may lead to God,
What right is mine to say
That he who fails to walk with me
Has missed the only way?

What right of mine to arrogate
Such grasp of finite mind,
And boast, while others vainly seek
The God I seek, and find?

How could the God I love and trust
Point out to only me
The way which travel, all men must,
Or die eternally?
I'm not so wise that He denies
The light to all save me,
While other hearts as true as mine
He loves with less degree.

So, if the path we tread should lead
Where bright cathedrals rise
Or weathered church, or rustic shrine
Point upward to the skies;
Each sincere traveler will arrive
Where lights of welcome shine,
And myriads will be there who walked
A different path than mine.
(*Oklahoma York Rite News*)

OF ALL KINDS

At a Masonic festivity the speaker divided Freemasons into six classes:

Emblem-wearing Masons, dues-paying Masons, knife-and-fork Masons, ritual-reciting Masons, ignorant Masons, and living-and-exemplifying Masons.

HEAVENLY CIRCUIT

Masonic speakers frequently use the following story to illustrate that we are known by our associates.

Saint Peter sent Saint Theresa down to earth to investigate conditions. She arrived in New York and after a week of investigation phoned Heaven long distance. Saint Peter answered. She said, "Saint Peter, this is Saint Theresa. I have been looking around New York and find it is a wicked city, and I would do something about it if I were you." He said, "I'll make a note. You go on to Chicago for a week." So she looked around in Chicago and reported that it, too, was a wicked city and that he should do something about it. Again, Saint Peter said that he would make a note and ordered her to go to Hollywood. Four weeks went by and no call from Saint Theresa. Finally, in the fifth week, the phone rang in Heaven, and Saint Peter said, "Hello." The voice at the other end of the line said, "Pete, Darling. This is Tessie!"

NAME AND NUMBER

The man being examined told the committee that he belonged to a lodge in Pennsylvania. They asked for the name of the lodge. He answered, "The lodge hasn't any name, only a number." The committee mulled this over for a bit, when the Mason revealed that he held dual membership in a lodge in Massachusetts. Then they asked for the Massachusetts lodge name and number. The man replied with the Lodge name only. It, like all Massachusetts lodges, didn't have a number. So one of the committee remarked, "Oh! so you had to join two lodges to get a name and number!"

DIRTY STORY

Another old favorite of Masonic speakers is this one:

A man came home from lodge and asked his wife if she had heard the story about the dirty window. She said, "No." "Well," he said, "I don't think you would see through it anyway."

She thought it was a good story so she called up her girl friend and asked her if she had heard the story about the window you couldn't see through. The girl friend said she had not. So the woman said, "It's too dirty, I can't tell it to you."

"I was lying there mulling over THE ROYAL ARCH MASON'S *subscription list when suddenly it hit me! By George, ol' Clyde's not a subscriber!"*

COCKTAIL PARTY? ? ?

One enterprising quasi-Masonic organization in its meeting notice listed the pre-meeting refreshment hour as the "Attitude Adjustment Period." (It was really a *dry* party! *Extra dry* martinis!)

THE OMNIPOTENT

The Master of a lodge in a small town, explaining to a meeting of the brethren that the Grand Master was prevented from keeping his promise to be present, said: "The head of our Order, the brother whose hand rules without restriction over tens of thousands of brethren in this state, our Powerful and Most Worshipful Grand Master, cannot be with us as his wife will not permit him to leave the house this evening."

WHAT'S IN A NAME?

Writing in the February, 1956 issue of the *Philalethes* magazine, Bro. A. L. Woody tells that a brother who was elected a member of that society received a letter of congratulation from a friend, because of his election to membership in a "stamp collector's society."

Probably there would be more money in a stamp collector's society (Philatelic) than in a student's society (Philalethes). At any rate there are more people interested in stamps than Masonic study —unfortunately for the fraternity.

Members of that society (Philalethes) will be surprised to know that the executive secretary, although a 32° and member of York Rite bodies, was buried in a Roman Catholic cemetery—at the request of the family!

HE WANTED IN

When Harold Painter of Sedalia began digging into the old records of Sedalia's first lodge, he discovered in the records of October 4, 1852 the following:

Ballot spread on the petition of Mr. X. N. Mfuxjdi for the first degree in Masonry—whereupon the petition was rejected.

Ballot spread a second time and the petition was rejected. Ordered that the initiation fee be refunded.

On motion the vote on the petition of Mr. X. N. Mfuxjdi was reconsidered. Ballots were spread on the petition for Mr. X. N. Mfuxdji and the said petition was rejected.

(The name is purposely concealed.)

It was quite apparent that the brethren *didn't want him!*

HIGH TWELVE!

A brave man struggling for the right
  Who death defies;
A good man overpowered by might
  And low he lies;
He dare not, can not, will not give
  Truth's cause away;
Yea, he would rather cease to live
  Than trust betray.
    High Twelve!

LOW TWELVE!

In darkness, in the dead of night,
  They make his grave;
And might has triumphed over right
  With none to save
The life which was the soul of duty
  Gone with a breath;
And he who was the type of beauty
  Pulseless in death.
    Low Twelve!

HIGH TWELVE!

Lo, Judah's Lion stoops to save;
  His strong right hand
Is reaching downward to the grave;
  The dead shall stand.
A grip, a word, he springs upright,
  The shadows fly;
He basks in heaven's eternal light
  No more to die.
    High Twelve!
      (McDOWELL)

DOGGONE

The minutes of Journeymen Masons Lodge No. 8, Edinburgh, Scotland, for April 9, 1868 record the following: During refreshment Brother B——— on going down the Hall was bitten by a dog belonging to Brother C——— which was the cause of much discussion. The R.W.M. proposed, seconded by the S.W. that in future no dog be allowed in any lodge meeting on the lodge premises, which was agreed to.

SECRETARY'S DREAM

I fell asleep the other night
 And while I had my snooze,
I dreamed each member stepped right up
 And promptly paid his dues.
But when I found 'twas but a dream
 I nearly threw a fit
It's up to you to make it true . . .
 SUGGESTION—Please Remit.

HOW TO SECURE LODGE ATTENDANCE

In the proceedings of a lodge in Munster, Ireland, December 8, 1726, it is recorded:

In a meeting of this lodge this day it was unanimously agreed that Mr. Herbert Phaires, a poor brother be every lodge night a Constant attend't of this lodge & that every night he so attends a brittish Crown be allow'd him for ye relief of his Distress'd Family.

But Brother Phaires' luck was not to continue, for we read in a later minute of the lodge that the said brother misbehaveing himself at the Grand Lodge . . . it was ordered that the above order Continue no longer in force.

The hen that had laid the golden egg had died!

"Steve's determined that a Mason is going to be the first to land on the moon!"

MASONIC WIDOWHOOD

The following letter to Abigail Van Buren of "Dear Abby" fame is a classic:

DEAR ABBY: My husband recently joined the Masonic lodge. Naturally I was very proud of him, but now it has presented a problem to us.

He tells me that this is a "secret organization" and he has given his word that he will tell no one about the secrets of the lodge.

Abby, in all the 18 years we have been married we have not kept any secrets from each other. I have cried, begged, threatened, and tried everything I could think of to make him tell me these "secrets" of his lodge, but he refuses.

How can an organization which is supposed to be dedicated to such high ideals create a barrier between a man and his wife? I'd appreciate your views.

WIFE OF A MASON

DEAR WIFE: Consider yourself fortunate to be married to a man whose word means something. And quit pestering him to reveal the lodge secrets or you'll lose your Mason by degrees.

SLIGHT ERROR

Henry Clausen, Past Grand Master of California, narrates that a nervous tyler in one of the lodges in his state, when he had to announce the arrival of the Grand Master, announced the arrival of the Great Architect of the Universe. "But I knew," adds the G.M., "that this could not be, for I am a lawyer."

QUALMLY WRITTEN

King David and King Solomon
Led merry, merry lives,
With many, many lady friends
And many, many wives;
But when old age crept over them,
With many, many qualms,
King Solomon wrote the Proverbs
And King David wrote the Psalms.

AMBITION

A private in the Army was being initiated. He was asked what he most desired. His reply was prompt: "The rank of sergeant."

RISE, FOLLOW YOUR CONDUCTOR

A lobster dealer was the Master of a small "Down East" Lodge in Maine. The candidate was a lobster fisherman. When asked in whom he put his trust, the candidate promptly answered, "Not in you, by God!"

NOT A SKULL SESSION

The Grand Master of Texas rendered a decision to the effect that "it is not permissible for a candidate to keep his skull cap on while taking the degrees."

NOT ENUFF TEA

In the *Masonic Chronicler,* May 19, 1945, appears an article headed "Immorality, Foundation of Masonry."

DO-GOODERS!

There is the incident of the Irish cop who stopped a carful of Shriners for speeding. When he saw that they were wearing fezes he said, "Oh! You're Shriners are you? Then I'll let you off this time because they do a lot of good. BUT if you were Masons I'd run you all in."

MIGHTIER THAN THE SWORD

M.W. Bro. Donald Gardner, a Maine Past Grand Master, tells of visiting a Lodge where a nervous Junior Deacon announced that the Tyler was "outside the sword with a drawn door in his hand."

LABOR PROBLEMS

Then there is the story about a good Brother who is a farmer in West Virginia. One morning he fell off his hay rack and broke his leg. He was rushed to the hospital in a nearby community where they gave him an anesthetic, set his leg, got it put in a cast, and then realized that they didn't have any bed for him. Every bed in the hospital was full except for one in the corner of the maternity ward. So they put him in that bed. He woke up sooner than they had expected him to, and began complaining about the way his leg hurt. One of the women in the maternity ward said, "Oh, you men make me tired—complaining about a broken leg! You ought to have a baby." He said, "Is that bad?" She replied, "Why if it wasn't for twilight sleep, we couldn't stand it!" "What's twilight sleep?" he asked. She said, "That's what they give you so you don't feel the pain." About that time the doctor came in and the farmer said, "Hey, Doc, I want some twilight sleep." The doctor said, "You can't have twilight sleep. That's for labor." The farmer, disgusted, said, "That's what's wrong with the country—everything for labor, nothing for the farmer!"

AN EDITOR'S WOES

An editor's job is no sinecure, and getting out a notice is no picnic. If we print jokes, folks say we are silly. If we don't they say we are too serious. If we publish original matter, they say we lack variety. If we publish things from other notices, we are too lazy to write. If we don't print contributions, we do not show appreciation. If we do print them, the paper is filled with junk. Like as not some fellow will say we swiped this from another notice.

He's right, we did.

(Lifted from *Masonry at Work,* a monthly publication of the Masonic bodies in Santa Barbara, California.)